RESPONSIBLE RESTRUCTURING

RESPONSIBLE RESTRUCTURING
Creative and Profitable Alternatives to Layoffs

Wayne F. Cascio
Graduate School of Business
University of Colorado–Denver

BERRETT-KOEHLER PUBLISHERS, INC.
San Francisco

SOCIETY FOR
HUMAN
RESOURCE
MANAGEMENT

Berrett-Koehler Publishers, Inc.
235 Montgomery Street, Suite 650
San Francisco, CA 94104-2916
Tel: (415) 288-0260   Fax: (415) 362-2512   www.bkconnection.com

Copublished by Berrett-Koehler Publishers and The Society for Human Resource Management.

ORDERING INFORMATION

Quantity sales. Special discounts are available on quantity purchases by corporations, associations, and others. For details, contact the "Special Sales Department" at the Berrett-Koehler address above.

Individual sales. Berrett-Koehler publications are available through most bookstores. They can also be ordered direct from Berrett-Koehler: Tel: (800) 929-2929; Fax: (802) 864-7626; www.bkconnection.com

Orders for college textbook/course adoption use. Please contact Berrett-Koehler: Tel: (800) 929-2929; Fax: (802) 864-7626.

Orders by U.S. trade bookstores and wholesalers. Please contact Publishers Group West, 1700 Fourth Street, Berkeley, CA 94710. Tel: (510) 528-1444; Fax (510) 528-3444.

Berrett-Koehler and the BK logo are registered trademarks of Berrett-Koehler Publishers, Inc.

Production Management: Michael Bass & Associates

The Society for Human Resource Management (SHRM) is the world's largest association devoted to human resource management. Representing more than 165,000 individual members, the Society serves the needs of HR professionals by providing the most essential and comprehensive set of resources available. As an influential voice, SHRM is committed to advancing the human resource profession to ensure that HR is essential and effective partner in developing and executing organizational strategy. Visit SHRM Online at **www.shrm.org.**

Printed in the United States of America

Berrett-Koehler books are printed on long-lasting acid-free paper. When it is available, we choose paper that has been manufactured by environmentally responsible processes. These may include using trees grown in sustainable forests, incorporating recycled paper, minimizing chlorine in bleaching, or recycling the energy produced at the paper mill.

Library of Congress Cataloging-in-Publication Data

Cascio, Wayne F.
    Responsible restructuring: creative and profitable alternatives to layoffs.
    Wayne F. Cascio
      p. cm.
    Includes bibliographical references and index.
    ISBN 1-57675-129-5
    1. Corporate reorganizations. 2. Corporate reorganizations—Case studies. 3. Employees—Training of. 4. Organizational effectiveness. 5. Employees—Dismissal of. I. Title.

HD58.8 .C365 2002
658.4′02—dc21   2002018501

First Edition
   05   04   03   02   10 9 8 7 6 5 4 3 2 1

To
Mom and Dad,
Joyce and Bill
Everything parents and siblings should be

Contents

List of Exhibits

Preface

This book is about changing managers' perceptions of employees from costs to be cut to assets to be developed. Almost two million American jobs were lost in 2001. In many cases, these job losses represented conscious decisions by managers to reduce the size of their workforces through layoffs or selling off unprofitable assets. In others, it almost surely was the result of "slash-and-burn" tactics that simply copied what competitors were doing.

Yet not all companies follow these approaches. This book highlights creative and profitable alternatives that some companies take in their approaches to restructuring and cutting costs. Those approaches are termed "responsible restructuring." The book shows that, especially in knowledge-based organizations, cutting people can often be disastrous, except as a last resort.

Consider this fact. Over the long term, any effort to develop an organization will encounter economic swings both up and down, as well as changes in markets, customers, products, services, and technology. I have found that "preventive planning" is a key difference between organizations that can deal with such changes in a systematic, orderly way, versus those that resort to knee-jerk reactions in order to respond swiftly (often through mass layoffs). Companies like Reflexite and Southwest Airlines (described in chapters 5 and 6, respectively) are good examples of preventive planners. Each has built a plan for restructuring into the overall economic plan for its business.

This book builds on the seminal publication I did in 1995 for the United States Department of Labor, entitled *Guide to Responsible Restructuring.* As I investigated the approaches that various companies, large and small, public and private, adopted in their efforts to restructure, what became obvious to me was that companies differed in terms of how they viewed their employees. Indeed, they almost seemed to separate themselves logically into two groups. One group, by far the larger of the two, saw employees as *costs to be cut.* The other, much smaller group saw employees as *assets to be developed.* Therein lay a major difference in the approaches they took to restructure their organizations.

- **Employees as costs to be cut**. These are the downsizers. They constantly ask themselves, "What is the minimum number of employees we need to run this company? What is the irreducible core number of employees the business requires?"

- **Employees as assets to be developed**. These are the responsible restructurers. They constantly ask themselves, "How can we change the way we do business, so that we can use the people we currently have more effectively?"

The downsizers see employees as commodities—like microchips or lightbulbs, interchangeable, substitutable, and disposable, if necessary. In contrast, responsible restructurers see employees as sources of innovation and renewal. They see in employees the potential to grow their businesses. Chapter 1 highlights these differences, puts the issue of restructuring into broad perspective, and examines the consequences of treating employees poorly versus the payoffs from treating them well.

Chapter 2 presents the results of an analysis of the financial consequences of alternative restructuring strategies used by 500 firms (Standard & Poor's 500, or the S&P 500) from 1982 to 2000. The S&P 500 is one of the most widely used benchmarks of the performance of U.S. equities. The study addressed two questions: "Are firms that downsize more profitable than those that don't, or more profitable than other firms in their own industries, in the year of the downsizing, as well as up to two years later?" and "Over the same time period, are stockholders better off investing in a portfolio of companies that downsize, as opposed to investing in companies that don't?" The answer to both questions is no. This is why it is reasonable to question the efficacy of downsizing as the preferred approach to restructuring, and to examine alternative approaches.

Chapter 3 explodes 13 myths about employment downsizing and presents the actual facts, based on systematic research. The myths address issues such as the profitability and productivity effects of employment downsizing; its effects on quality as well as on the morale, workload, and commitment of survivors; the security of jobs at firms that are doing well; and the health consequences of layoffs.

Chapter 4 presents the case for restructuring and the introduction of "high-performance work practices." The latter include practices such as skills training and continuous learning, information sharing, employee participation in the design and implementation of work processes, flattened organizational structures, labor–management partnerships, compensation linked to employee skills and organizational performance, and customer satisfaction—as defined by customers. The chapter presents compelling evidence to support the conclusion that high-performance work practices have important, meaningful effects on a firm's financial and nonfinancial performance indicators and that the most effective employment relationships are those in which open-ended inducements provided by employers are balanced by open-ended contributions from employees.

Chapter 5 presents 10 alternative approaches to responsible restructuring, using as illustrations Charles Schwab & Co., Compaq Computer, Cisco, Accenture, Motorola, Reflexite, Intel, Minnesota Mining and Manufacturing Company (3M), ChevronTexaco, Acxiom, Sage Software, Louisiana-Pacific Corporation, Philips Electronics Singapore, and Procter & Gamble. The chapter describes the specific practices these firms use to demonstrate their commitment to their people as assets to be developed rather than as costs to be cut. Even when cuts are necessary, firms such as these use practices that promote goodwill and loyalty, both among those who leave as well as among those who stay.

Chapter 6 highlights a small group of firms, public as well as private, large as well as small, that have implemented no-layoff policies, and it describes specific employment and business practices at three no-layoff companies: Lincoln Electric, SAS Institute, and Southwest Airlines. The chapter emphasizes that there is virtue in the stability of employment and that there is a no-layoff payoff.

Chapter 7 is a capstone chapter that illustrates what to do—and what not to do—when restructuring responsibly. It points out common mistakes that companies make when restructuring, along with advice on how to avoid those mistakes. It is a step-by-step guide to responsible restructuring that builds on all of the research and practical experiences presented elsewhere in the book.

Wayne F. Cascio
Golden, Colorado
June, 2002

Acknowledgments

Like many other books, this one is the product of inputs and ideas from many people. I have had the benefit of wise counsel from a variety of individuals. Two of my colleagues in the Business School at the University of Colorado–Denver have greatly influenced my thinking and my research. Cliff Young in marketing and Jim Morris in finance have collaborated with me in a long-term research program to investigate the financial effects of employment downsizing. Our interdisciplinary team is living testimony to the fact that "the whole is greater than the sum of its parts."

I would also like to acknowledge the detailed, constructive feedback that I received from five hardworking reviewers of the manuscript: Jim Evers, Marsha Daszko, Daniel Lowery, Richard Lynch, and Mark Stewart. Their helpful comments and questions forced me to clarify and, in some instances, to rethink, many of my ideas. I am deeply grateful to them and know that their input considerably improved the manuscript. In the final analysis, however, any errors or misstatements are mine, and I bear responsibility for them.

Finally, I would like to acknowledge the steadfast support and encouragement I have received throughout this project from Steve Piersanti, president and publisher of Berrett-Koehler Publishers, Inc. Steve has been a pleasure to work with, as have other members of the team at Berrett-Koehler, including Jeevan Sivasubramaniam and Heather Vaughan.

1

Restructuring in Perspective

Many firms are restructuring by downsizing their work-forces. Those most likely to take that approach see employees as costs to be cut rather than assets to be developed.

Picture this scenario. You are the chief executive officer at Grayson McBerry—a medium-sized securities trading firm headquartered in New York, with branches in most major cities in North America, Europe, Asia, and Australia. The second quarter just ended, and your firm's year-over-year revenues are off 52 percent. Its stock price is down almost 30 percent from the beginning of the year, and your best guess is that there will be little improvement until the first quarter of next year. You know you have got to do something to improve the financial condition of the firm, but what might that "something" be? As you study the latest set of quarterly reports, two competing considerations cross your mind.

On the one hand, you know that Grayson McBerry relies on the knowledge and creativity of its employees to a very great extent in conducting its business and in generating innovative products and services for its customers. You know that the firm's employees have enabled it to generate unparalleled results over the past decade and that customers are very loyal to the employees with whom they deal regularly. On the other hand, employees are also your most significant source of operating expenses, for compensation costs account for fully 52 cents of every dollar of sales.

You are well aware that firms have taken alternative approaches to coping with downturns in their businesses. For example, you know that in 2001 your competitor, Merrill Lynch, hit a rough patch. Its net earnings were off 39 percent from the previous year, and its stock price had fallen almost 32 percent since the beginning of the year. In an effort to cut costs, chief executive officer Stanley O'Neal announced plans to cut roughly one of every six employees from its worldwide workforce, as many as 10,000 out of 62,800 employees. Merrill took a $2.2 billion pretax charge in the fourth quarter of 2001 to do that.[1] In contrast, Charles Schwab & Co. faced circumstances similar to those of Merrill Lynch, and while ultimately it did cut 23 percent of its workforce of 26,000 in 2001, it used layoffs only as a last resort, not as a first step.[2] As a third example, you ponder the strategy of investment bank Lehman Brothers, Inc. At the same time as rivals were laying off thousands of employees to cut costs, chief executive officer Richard Fuld insisted that he would keep his staff intact and even hire new talent![3]

You know that outside your industry, some firms have steadfastly refused to lay off employees. Leading advertising agencies, such as Wieden & Kennedy, Publicis Groupe's Saatchi & Saatchi, Omnicom Group's TBWA/Chiat/Day, and WPP Group of London have eschewed layoffs in favor of salary cuts, hiring freezes, and reduced expenses.[4] In aircraft manufacturing, while Boeing announced as many as 30,000 layoffs after the September 11, 2001, terrorist attacks left the global airline industry reeling, rival Airbus vowed not to cut jobs, choosing instead to reduce headcount by 1,000 from 45,000 through attrition and other cost-cutting measures.[5]

As the economy weakened, other firms actually seized the opportunity to strengthen their competitive positions through strategies such as price cuts (Dell Computer), capital expansion (Wal-Mart), aggressive marketing (Sara Lee, Wendy's), and acquisitions (Best Buy).[6]

To be sure, senior executives at firms both large and small have made difficult choices about strategies to cope with a downturn in business. Some have decided to cut costs, often by cutting employees. Others have taken a different tack, cutting costs without cutting people, cutting people as a last resort, or even adopting growth strategies to solidify their competitive positions. What will you do at Grayson McBerry?

To many senior executives, the choice is clear: cut costs by reducing headcount. Firms often take these actions in the name of "restructuring." Oh, yes, they use a variety of euphemisms to soften the blow—"rightsizing," "repositioning," "delayering," "downsizing," "retrenchment"—but it seems that the result is always the same. Employees lose their jobs. They get "ICEd" through Involuntary Career Events. Is this outcome preordained? Is it written somewhere that when firms restructure it has to turn out like this? To put this issue into perspective, let's consider the economic logic that drives layoff decisions.

THE ECONOMIC LOGIC THAT DRIVES EMPLOYMENT DOWNSIZING

What makes employment downsizing such a compelling strategy to firms worldwide? The economic rationale is straightforward. It begins with the premise that there really are only two ways to make money in business: either you cut costs, or you increase revenues. Which is more predictable, future costs or future revenues? Anyone who makes monthly mortgage payments knows that future costs are far more predictable than future revenues. Payroll expenses represent fixed costs, so by cutting payroll, other things remaining equal, one should reduce overall expenses.

As an example, consider Merrill Lynch, which, as we noted earlier, implemented massive layoffs in late 2001 in an effort to reduce its expenses. Before the layoffs, Merrill devoted fully 54 cents of every dollar it took in to employee compensation, compared to an estimated 49 cents at Goldman Sachs & Co. and 52 cents at Morgan Stanley Dean Witter & Co.[7] Reduced expenses translate into increased earnings, and earnings drive stock prices. Higher stock prices make investors and analysts happy. The key phrase is "other things remaining equal." As we shall see, other things often do not remain equal, and therefore the anticipated benefits of employment downsizing do not always materialize.

DIRECT AND INDIRECT COSTS OF LAYOFFS

Although layoffs are intended to reduce costs, some costs may in fact increase. The material below summarizes these costs.

DIRECT AND INDIRECT COSTS OF LAYOFFS

Direct Costs	Indirect Costs
Severance pay, in lieu of notice	Recruiting and employment costs of new hires
Accrued vacation and sick pay	Low morale; risk-averse survivors
Supplemental unemployment benefits	Increase in unemployment tax rate
Outplacement	Lack of staff when economy rebounds; training and retraining
Pension and benefit payouts	Potential lawsuits from aggrieved employees
Administrative processing costs	Heightened insecurity; reduced productivity
Costs of rehiring former employees	Loss of institutional memory and trust in management

It doesn't have to be this way. There is an alternative, one known as "responsible restructuring." This little book describes this alternative approach, illustrates its advantages over "slash-and-burn" layoff tactics, and provides examples of firms that restructure responsibly. Responsible restructuring is not some mystical, obscure set of practices. On the contrary, it is eminently practical and doable, but it does require a break with traditional thinking, as the next sections illustrate. Let's begin by defining our terms.

Organizational restructuring refers to planned changes in a firm's organizational structure that affect its use of people. For example, General Electric scrapped the vertical structure that was in place in its lighting business and replaced it with a horizontal structure characterized by over 100 different processes and programs. Xerox currently develops new products through the use of multidisciplinary teams; the vertical approach that had been used over the years is gone. This is restructuring through "delayering." The objective? Improved financial performance through increased productivity and efficiency.[8]

Such restructuring often results in workforce reductions that may be accomplished through mechanisms such as attrition, early retirements, voluntary severance agreements, or layoffs. The term *layoffs* is used sometimes as if it were synonymous with *downsizing*, but downsizing is a broad term that can include any number of combinations of reductions in a firm's use of assets—financial, physical, human, or information assets.[9] Layoffs are the same as employment downsizing.

Employment downsizing, in turn, is not the same thing as organizational decline. Downsizing is an intentional, proactive management strategy, whereas decline is an environmental or organizational phenomenon that occurs involuntarily and results in erosion of an organization's resource base.[10] As an example of decline, the advent of digital photography, disposable cameras, and other imaging products signaled a steep decline in the demand for the kind of instant photographic cameras and films that Polaroid had pioneered in the 1940s. On October 12, 2001, Polaroid was forced to declare bankruptcy.[11]

To put the issue of *organizational* restructuring into perspective, it is important to emphasize what it is not. It is not *financial* restructuring, which refers to a change in the configuration of a firm's financial or physical assets, and its financing of debt or equity. Nor does it imply a change in the configuration of a firm's information resources, such as downsizing or upsizing its information technology infrastructure. As noted earlier, organizational restructuring refers to planned changes in organizational structure that affect the use of people.

IS RESTRUCTURING A BAD THING TO DO?

No. Kodak, an old-line company that sold cameras and film in the early 20th century, is struggling to turn around its businesses in a digital era. Some form of restructuring is healthy—and needed. Likewise, companies that find themselves saddled with nonperforming assets or consistently unprofitable subsidiaries should consider unloading them to buyers who can make better use of those assets. Sometimes the process of restructuring leads to layoffs and losses of jobs, especially when the jobs relied on old technology that is no longer commercially viable. This was the case in the newspaper industry when most metropolitan dailies switched from hot to cold (computer-based) typesetting. There simply was no longer a need for compositors, a trade that had been handed down from generation to generation. However, indiscriminate "slash-and-burn" tactics, such as across-the-board downsizing of employees, seldom leads to long-term gains in productivity, profits, or stock prices, as we shall see. There is another way, and that way is known as responsible restructuring.

RESPONSIBLE RESTRUCTURING— WHAT IS IT?

In 1995, I wrote a publication for the U.S. Department of Labor entitled *Guide to Responsible Restructuring*.[12] As I investigated the approaches that various companies, large and small, public and private, adopted in their efforts to restructure, what became obvious to me was that companies differed in terms of how they viewed their employees. Indeed, they almost seemed to separate themselves logically into two groups. One group, by far the larger of the two, saw employees as *costs to be cut*. The other, much smaller group of firms, saw employees as *assets to be developed*. Therein lay a major difference in the approaches they took to restructure their organizations.

- **Employees as costs to be cut**—executives at these organizations are the downsizers. They constantly ask themselves, "What is the minimum number of employees we need to run this company? What is the irreducible core number of employees the business requires?"

- **Employees as assets to be developed**—executives at these organizations are the responsible restructurers. They constantly ask themselves, "How can we change the way we do business, so that we can use the people we currently have more effectively?"

The downsizers see employees as commodities—like paper clips or lightbulbs—interchangeable and substitutable, one for another. This is a "plug-in" mentality: plug them in when you need them; pull the plug when you no longer need them. In contrast, responsible restructurers see employees as sources of innovation and renewal. They see in employees the potential to grow their businesses.

We will present several examples of responsible restructuring, but first let us consider the current state of employment downsizing.

EMPLOYMENT DOWNSIZING— THE JUGGERNAUT CONTINUES[13]

The "job churning" (movement of people from one organization to another) in the labor market that characterized the 1990s has not let up. In fact, its pace has accelerated. However, the free-agent mentality of the late 1990s that motivated some people to leave one employer so that they could make 5 percent more at another is over. Layoffs are back—and with a vengeance. Thus, in 2001, companies in the United States announced layoffs of 1.96 million workers, with firms such as American Express, Lucent, Hewlett-Packard, and Dell Computer conducting multiple rounds in the same year. Corporations announced 999,000 job cuts between September 11, 2001, and February 1, 2002, alone![14]

Manufacturing lost the bulk of the jobs (more than 800,000), but services were not exempt either, dropping more than 100,000. Most such jobs were in the travel industry, with airlines (United, Delta, American, Continental, USAirways Group, Northwest, and America West) leading the way. Boeing shed 38,000 workers, and Starwood Hotels & Resorts another 12,000. More than 600,000 high-technology jobs were lost in 2001, along with another 50,000+ in the U.S. securities industry.[15]

Medium- and large-sized companies announce most layoffs, and they involve *all* levels of employees, top to bottom. A study by Bain & Company's Worldwide Strategy Practice reported that in 2000, for example, 22 percent of the CEOs of the largest publicly traded companies either lost their jobs or retired, as opposed to just 13 percent in 1999.[16] CEOs at firms such as Ford Motor, UAL, British Telecom, Ericsson, and Providian were either ousted or re-signed in 2001.[17] Morgan Stanley estimates that about 80 percent of the U.S. layoffs involve white-collar, well-educated employees. According to Morgan Stanley's chief economist, that's because 75 percent of the 12.3 million new jobs created between 1994 and 2000 were white-collar jobs. What the companies created, they are now taking away.

THE HUMAN AND FINANCIAL TOLL

Numbers alone are sterile and abstract. In fact, involuntary layoffs are traumatic. They exact a devastating toll on workers and communities. Lives are shattered, people become bitter and angry, and the added emotional and financial pressure can create family problems. "Survivors," workers who remain on the job, can be left without loyalty or motivation. Their workplaces are more stressful, political, and cutthroat than before the downsizing. Local economies and services (e.g., human services agencies, charitable organizations) become strained under the impact to the community.

The fact is, layoffs and heavy debt loads (which reached an all-time high in 2001, along with personal bankruptcies) are hitting families hard and ratcheting up stress levels. Employee assistance counselors have seen a marked increase in "crisis" calls involving problems such as online affairs, addictions in adolescents, and spousal abuse. Counselors say spousal abuse is occurring more and more against men.[18] Says Richard Chaifetz, chair and CEO of Compsych, the world's largest privately held employee assistance program, "People feel like they had the rug pulled out from under them; they were living in a fantasy world."[19]

Over the past decade or so, the same scenario has become depressingly familiar to millions of people, from former dot.com employees to those of former energy-trading company Enron. For example, at the time of Enron's bankruptcy filing in late 2001, it was the seventh largest firm in the United States in terms of revenues. When the dismissal notices came, some employees had as little as 30 minutes to collect their things and get out. Not surprisingly, many are bitter. As one former employee said, "You were on top of the world when you were there. I thought I'd be there a long time."[20]

For those who still have jobs, their incomes, hours, and bonuses, like those of executives at Ford Motor Company and Sun Microsystems, may be cut, in an effort to avoid more layoffs. Companies are well aware of the effects of these financial problems. Human resource professionals figure that when workers worry about family finances, they waste 13 percent of the workday calling creditors and other distractions. Money woes also lead to medical problems, lower productivity, and to increased absenteeism and accidents. What about the managers who do all the firing? Their health suffers too. A recent study conducted at 45 American hospitals found that executives ran twice as much risk of a heart attack in the week after firing someone.[21]

These forces often culminate in a phenomenon known as burnout. *Burnout* is a gradual process of loss during which the mismatch between the needs of the person and the demands of the job grows ever greater. Ask people what it's like to feel burned out, and you are likely to hear the following:[22]

> "I'm frustrated! It's getting impossible to do a good job, and the situation just keeps getting worse."
>
> "I've lost my enthusiasm for work I really liked."
>
> "I have lots of anger, and nowhere to take it."
>
> "I'm scared; is the job going to last?"
>
> "I am getting more unhappy and depressed every day on the job, and questioning whether I should stick with it."
>
> "I'm feeling overwhelmed, overloaded, overworked—and trapped. There's no way out."

Research indicates that each person expresses burnout in a unique way, but the basic themes are the same:

- **An erosion of engagement with the job**. What started out as important, meaningful, fascinating work becomes unpleasant, unfulfilling, and meaningless.

- **An erosion of emotions**. The positive feelings of enthusiasm, dedication, security, and enjoyment fade away and are replaced by anger, anxiety, and depression.

- **A problem of fit between the person and the job.** Individuals see this imbalance as a personal crisis, but it is really the workplace that is in trouble.[23]

Burnout often causes people to quit their jobs. Others are laid off. This raises an interesting question—namely, what happens to displaced workers? The Labor Department's latest biennial survey of workers who lost long-term jobs (held for at least three years) provides a hint. Conducted early in 2000 when the economy was still red-hot, its results indicate that even in the best of times, many displaced workers suffer lost earnings (see Exhibit 1).

EXHIBIT 1   Status in Early 2000 of Full-Timers Who Lost Permanent Jobs in 1997–1998

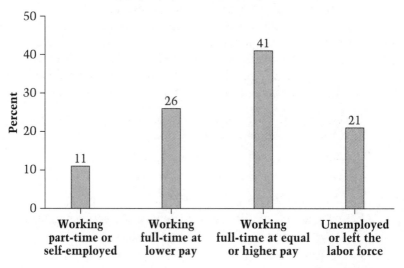

A year or two after being laid off, 21 percent of former full-timers either were still unemployed or had given up looking for work, and another 11 percent were self-employed, working part-time, or doing unpaid family work. Nearly 40 percent of reemployed workers had to change occupations to find work. Moreover, 39 percent of those back on full-time payrolls were receiving less pay than at their previous jobs, with more than half of those suffering wage declines of at least 20 percent. (After adjusting for inflation, the declines were even larger.)

While these figures might be worrisome, they probably represent a best-case scenario because the survey was conducted when the economy was hot. The fate of people who lose jobs during periods of falling employment and plummeting profits will be far more onerous.

The outlook for displaced workers in their 50s and early 60s may be even more uncertain. That's the age category that was hit hardest in the layoff surges of the early and mid-1990s. It's also the category that many baby boomers have recently entered.[24] The experience of workers in these age groups is not encouraging. Thus, only about half of over-55 workers displaced in 1993–1994 were reemployed by February 1996.[25]

THE EFFECT OF POOR LABOR RELATIONS ON PRODUCT QUALITY

Do workers exert more effort and due diligence if they feel they are treated fairly, and with dignity and respect? Conversely, does a poor labor relations climate affect product quality? Both economic and psychological research suggests that the answer is yes.[26] Unfortunately, the consequences may be deadly, as indicated in a recent analysis by two Princeton University economists of Bridgestone/Firestone tire production at the firm's Decatur, Illinois, plant when labor and management were battling.[27]

When a previous contract expired on April 1, 1994, employees worked for three months without a contract before going on strike. In negotiations, Bridgestone/Firestone broke with its industry by moving from an 8-hour to a 12-hour shift that would rotate between days and nights, as well as cutting pay for new hires by 30 percent, cutting wages for most job classifications by $5.34 per hour to about $12 per hour, reducing incentive pay for piecework, cutting two weeks of vacations for senior workers, and requiring hourly workers to contribute to their health care costs. The United Rubber Workers union that represented the workers proposed that the company follow the master pattern agreement set with Goodyear, which called for no wage increases other than cost-of-living adjustments. It is noteworthy that the company insisted on such large concessions during a period when the overall economy was growing.

Using replacements, the company imposed 12-hour shifts and kept production going. The union workers surrendered in May 1995, returning under the terms originally demanded by Bridgestone/Firestone. Although the strike officially ended in May 1995, the labor dispute continued until a final settlement was reached in December 1996. For nearly three years, therefore, from April 1994 to December 1996, union workers at the Decatur plant either were on strike or working without a contract. During this period, tires were produced by 1,048 replacement workers, union members who crossed the picket line, management, and re-called strikers.

The Princeton analysis is compelling because three different sets of data all point the same way. Firestone tires made in Decatur during the labor strife were 376 percent more likely to prompt a complaint to the National Highway Transportation Safety

Administration than tires made at two comparison plants. The two plants were Firestone's nonunion plant in Wilson, North Carolina, and its unionized plant in Joliette, Quebec, which had a 1995 strike but did not use replacement workers. During times of labor peace, Decatur tires were 14 percent *less* likely to prompt a complaint.

Second, customers with tires made in Decatur during the dispute were more than 250 percent as likely to seek compensation from Firestone for property damage or injury blamed on faulty tires than were customers of tires made there during more peaceful times. Third, tires made in Decatur during the labor dispute did worse on laboratory stress tests that Firestone conducted when the tires were produced than those made at other times or at other plants. The consequences were lethal, for the report concluded that more than 40 lives were lost as a result of the excessive number of problem tires produced in Decatur during the labor dispute.

Apparently the problem tires were not the result of production by inexperienced replacement workers. Rather, it appears that it was something about the chemistry between the replacements and the recalled strikers. Why? Analysis of monthly tire production revealed that there was no surge in problem tires when replacement workers were making them, adjusting for lower production volumes. The problems were with tires made in 1994 following tough company demands on the union and, again, after the strikers returned in May 1995 without a contract to work alongside workers who had crossed the picket line.

Is there a lesson to be learned in all of this? According to one observer, "squeezing workers, even in an age of weakened unions, can be bad management, especially when employers abruptly change the rules. A company can shut a plant and successfully hire lower-paid workers elsewhere. And if management convinces workers that the alternative to wage cuts is unemployment, workers may go along. But brute force can backfire, and the consequences can be severe."[28]

THE PAYOFF FROM TREATING EMPLOYEES AS ASSETS

Each year *Fortune* magazine publishes lists of top companies: the "100 Best Companies to Work For," "America's Most Admired

Companies," the "Global Most Admired Companies," and the best companies for Asians, African Americans, Hispanics, and Native Americans. Does it matter if a company's name appears on one of these lists? As one international observer recently commented: "'A good place to work' is one of the criteria for getting on the 'most admired companies' lists around the world. Analysts, investors, customers, potential employees and the community frequently use this quality to make judgments about the company, its stock and its future value."[29] Do these companies do better in the marketplace than those who are not listed?

A recent analysis by Hewitt Associates of the financial performance of publicly traded companies featured on the "100 Best" list versus the broad market and similar organizations that did not make the list found some compelling results. "Best Companies" have higher average stock returns, higher operating performance (ratio of operating income to assets), higher returns on assets, and higher returns on capital employed. In addition, they receive almost twice the number of job applications (1.9 times) compared to companies in their industries that are not on the list, and they also have much lower employee turnover (12.6 percent vs. 26 percent).[30]

Consider another analysis that compared the stock market performance of the top ten firms versus the bottom ten firms in the list of America's Most Admired Companies. From 1995 to 2000, the average total return on common stock for the top 10 firms was 41.4 percent; for the bottom 10 firms it was minus 23 percent. Compare these returns to that of a well-known benchmark of the performance of U.S. equities, the Standard & Poor's 500 (S&P 500), whose average return was 16.5 percent.[31]

The Hay Group surveyed the Global Most Admired companies, as well as their peers who did not make the list, about the performance measures they use to chart the progress of their companies. Hay Group vice president Mel Stark noted, "High-performing companies do walk the walk when it comes to performance measures. It's clear that they are seriously committed to the human elements that contribute to their success."[32]

Here's a third example. *Working Mother* magazine annually ranks companies based on pay, opportunities for women to advance, child care, flexibility, and other family-friendly benefits (e.g., maternity leaves) and work-life supports, such as management training on work-life issues. Is the presence of work-life policies related to performance in the marketplace? When the public companies that made the *Working Mother* "Best" list were assembled into a stock portfolio and their price performance compared to that of the S&P 500 Index, the "best companies for women to work for," on average, consistently outperformed the index over the three-year period 1996 through 1998, a time period of extraordinary returns for the S&P 500 Index.[33]

In its 2002 list of the "100 Best Companies to Work For," *Fortune* included these snippets of information about a dozen firms in different industries:

- **Container Store** (retailer of boxes): Workers are enthusiastic about good pay (salespeople average $36,256), great benefits (100 percent match for 401[k] up to 4 percent of pay), and respect (94 percent of those surveyed feel they make a difference).

- **Fenwick & West** (law): Whipped by declining fortunes of its high-tech clients, it laid off 47 people, but gave them four months of full pay. New recruits were offered an average of $62,500 not to join the firm.

- **Graniterock** (construction): This firm sends positive customer comments about employees home for families to read. Its safety record is twice as good as the industry average, and workers get 12 massages per year.

- **JM Family Enterprises** (auto distribution): Post–September 11, 2001, founder Jim Moran told an all-company gathering, "We're a family. We've got to make sure we do whatever we can do not to lay off one single associate." And they did not.

- **American Century Investments** (financial services): Clobbered by the decline on Wall Street, it avoided massive layoffs. Only 75 people were let go, and they walked out with one month's pay for each year of service.

- **Valassis** (printing): This company invites workers to provide suggestions at briefing sessions. As orders fell after September 11, 2001, employees offered ways to cut costs, such as using more uncoated paper, and avoided layoffs.

- **Continental Airlines** (airlines): Workers suffered as September 11, 2001, rocked the airlines, but Continental tried to do right by them. It furloughed 4,000 people who got severance payments, the chance to transfer, or the promise of a job when times get better.

- **Wegmans** (groceries): When 315 jobs were phased out recently, displaced workers were offered the option of another job without any cut in pay or leaving with severance up to one year's pay.

- **First Tennessee** (banking): This company declares, "Employees come first. Not customers, not shareholders."

- **Ernst & Young** (accounting): This firm was judged a "friendly place to work" by 88 percent of those surveyed. Employees also think management treats minorities, gays, and women fairly. A quarter of the new partner class last year was female.

- **Marriott International** (hotels): After September 11, 2001, it enhanced early-retirement packages and cut managers' pay, but layoffs happened anyway.

- **Texas Instruments** (technology): Ninety-two percent of employees surveyed say they are proud to tell others they work here.

There is a common thread that runs through all of these companies, as well as the others recognized as good places to work. Every one of them views its employees as assets to be developed rather than as costs to be cut.

We noted earlier that restructuring, including employment downsizing, is driven by the need to improve productivity and efficiency, whether in response to organizational decline or as a means to enhance profitability when the corporation is performing well. We assume that decision makers understand the relationship between their approach to restructuring and future financial performance so that restructuring can be used as a rational, predictable tool for manipulating that performance. Is that a reasonable assumption to make? The next chapter presents some surprising findings about the long-term financial consequences of alternative restructuring methods.

2

The Financial Consequences of Alternative Restructuring Strategies

Employment downsizing is not the only way to restructure, although it certainly is a popular strategy. Managers often assume that it will lead to improvements in financial performance. The research presented here tests that assumption.

Are companies better off financially after restructuring? To address this question, two colleagues (one from finance, one from marketing) and I studied financial and employment data from companies in the Standard & Poor's 500 (the S&P 500) from 1982 to 1994. The S&P 500 is one of the most widely used benchmarks of the performance of U.S. equities. It represents leading companies in leading industries, and consists of 500 stocks chosen for their market size, liquidity, and industry group representation. Each stock's weight in the index is proportionate to its market value (stock price times number of shares outstanding). However, the stocks that comprise the index do not remain constant over time. In fact, from its inception in 1926 through September 15, 2000, 1,001 companies exited the S&P 500, the overwhelming majority as a result of mergers and acquisitions.[1]

Our purpose was to examine the relationships between changes in employment and long-term financial performance. Specifically, we measured changes in profitability (return on assets, or ROA) and the total return on common stock (dividends plus price appreciation). We categorized companies based on their level of change in employment and their level of change in plant and equipment (assets), and we observed performance from one year before to two years after the employment-change events.[2]

Our primary interest was the change in employment from one year to the next. Over the period of the study, however, some companies increased their levels of employment, others decreased their levels of employment, and many did both at various times. Moreover, some changed their employment through hiring and/or layoffs, while others reported employment changes that must have resulted from purchasing or selling plants or divisions. For example, suppose a firm reports a 10 percent reduction in employment from 1990 to 1991. That reduction in employment could be due to a decision to lay off employees without any reduction in assets, or it might be due to a decision to sell off unprofitable plants or divisions. The former set of circumstances represents a pure employment downsizing, while the latter represents a downsizing with divestiture. Each of these scenarios might have a different impact on a firm's financial performance. For example, the market might react differently over time to a divestiture than it does to an employment downsizing. By considering changes in employment *relative to* changes in assets, we were able to account for most of the effects of changes in each of them.

To control for the varying impacts of employment increases or decreases, and for changes due to variability in employment per se, versus asset acquisitions or divestitures, we classified each firm into one of seven mutually exclusive categories in each period of the study:

- **Employment Downsizers**: companies in which the decline in employment is greater than 5 percent and the decline in plant and equipment is less than 5 percent
- **Downsizing by reducing assets (Asset Downsizers)**: companies with a decline in employment greater than 5 percent and a decline in plant and equipment that exceeds the change in employment by at least 5 percent
- **Combination employment and asset reduction (Combination Downsizers)**: companies that reduce the number of employees by more than 5 percent but do not fit into either of the two prior categories
- **Stable Employers**: companies with changes in employment between plus or minus 5 percent

Although our focus was on downsizing, we also categorized companies based on their employment growth. To do that, we defined three more categories relating to employment upsizing:

- **Employment Upsizers**: companies in which the increase in employment is greater than 5 percent and the increase in plant and equipment is less than 5 percent

- **Upsizing by acquiring assets (Asset Upsizers):** companies with an increase in employment of 5 percent or greater and an increase in plant and equipment that exceeds the change in employment by at least 5 percent

- **Combination employment and asset increase (Combination Upsizers)**: companies that increase employment by more than 5 percent but do not fit into either of the other upsizing categories

We recognize that our classification of companies as Downsizers, Upsizers, or Stable Employers is somewhat arbitrary. For stable employers, we chose ±5 percent, relative to a base year, as a cutoff point. We considered 3 percent and 10 percent as alternative limits, but we concluded that using ±3 percent would include in the employment downsizing categories too many companies that could have reduced their employment that much merely through attrition and not through a conscious downsizing decision. On the other hand, using ±10 percent excluded from the downsizing categories many larger companies that had announced and implemented employment downsizings that were quite large in terms of the absolute numbers of employees affected.

RESULTS OF THE 1982–1994 STUDY

Impact on Financial Performance

We found no significant, consistent evidence that employment downsizing led to improved financial performance, as measured by *return on assets* (ROA) and industry-adjusted ROA.[a] It is important

---

[a]A standard measure of the financial performance of a firm is ROA, measured as operating income before depreciation, interest, and taxes divided by total assets. Any changes in the firm's performance that result from employment downsizing should show up in this measure.

EXHIBIT 2   Industry-Adjusted Return on Assets for Downsizing Companies

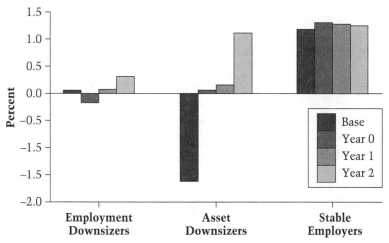

to assess results relative to results for the same industry in which a firm competes, because firms in the same industry face similar economic and competitive conditions. We found that on average, Employment Downsizers were less profitable in the year of the downsizing (the base year) than either the Upsizers or Stable Employers. They remained that way for the subsequent two years. It was only by the end of year 2 that the ROA of Employment Downsizers was slightly higher than that of their industry, but it still fell below that of Stable Employers. Only Asset Downsizers showed a significant increase in their profitability relative to Stable Employers and their industries by the end of year 2. These results are shown graphically in Exhibit 2.[3]

Thus, performance improvement appears to depend on the reason for the downsizing. The firms that engaged in aggressive asset restructuring improved their profitability and outperformed their industries, while those that did not tended to experience declines in their profitability and did not outperform their industries. This suggests that simply laying off employees to improve financial performance may not lead to the intended improvement in a firm's financial performance if the layoffs are not accompanied by thoughtful restructuring of the firm's assets.

A striking feature of our findings was that employment downsizing had a negligible impact on profitability when compared to the size of the layoffs. Employment Downsizers reduced their workforces by an average of 10.5 percent, but they failed to increase their profitability (ROA) until the end of year 2. Even then, they were able to attain an ROA that was only 0.3 percent above their industry average, which is not significant, considering the high percentage of layoffs. No matter how many employees they lay off, employers that downsize always seem to trail the performance of Stable Employers. Nevertheless, companies continue to announce large layoffs, assuming that employment downsizing will increase profits.

Impact on Stock Performance

The second measure of performance used in the study was the total return on common stock. We tracked the stock return for companies in each of the seven categories from one year prior to the employment changes through the second year after the employment changes. We then compared the returns to the Stable Employers and to each company's industry. The results were very clear. In the year that they increased employment, the three categories of Upsizers generated stock returns that were 50 percent higher than the Stable Employers (0.27 vs. 0.18) did. Over the three-year period, upsizing companies as a group generated cumulative stock returns that were 20 percentage points higher than the Stable Employers did. On the other hand, the downsizing companies as a group performed no better than the Stable Employers over the same three-year period.

We adjusted each company's stock return for industry performance by subtracting the average industry stock return from the company's return. The resulting industry-adjusted return implicitly takes account of risk because the industry-average return will, itself, include a risk premium for the systematic risk of that particular industry. Thus, any return that is significantly different from that of the industry is a return that is in excess of the return required for that industry's level of risk. As it turned out, none of the categories exhibited returns that were significantly different from those of their industries.

EXTENSION AND UPDATE FROM 1995 TO 2000

To date, scholars have not found consistent relationships between downsizing and financial performance,[4] but they have used different analytical approaches, and generally have not examined performance over multiyear periods. However, one exception is research reported in the 2001 book *Good to Great*, which identified companies that sustained superior financial performance for 15 or more years. Good-to-great companies generally avoided layoffs:

> The good-to-great companies rarely used head-count lopping as a tactic and almost never used it as a primary strategy. . . . Six of the eleven good-to-great companies recorded zero layoffs from ten years before the breakthrough date all the way through 1998, and four others reported only one or two layoffs.
>
> In contrast, we found layoffs used five times more frequently in the comparison companies than in the good-to-great companies. Some of the comparison companies had an almost chronic addiction to layoffs and restructurings.
>
> It would be a mistake—a tragic mistake, indeed—to think that the way you ignite a transition from good to great is by wantonly swinging the ax on vast numbers of hardworking people. Endless restructuring and mindless hacking were never part of the good-to-great model.[5]

In an effort to provide a large-sample estimate of the relationship between downsizing and financial performance, my colleague Clifford Young and I updated our earlier analysis to include results through the end of 2000.[6] Using the same approach as in the previous study, we observed a total of 6,418 occurrences of changes in employment for S&P 500 companies over the 18-year period from 1982 through 2000. Exhibit 3 shows the distribution of cases across the various employment-change categories from the year of the announcement (year 0) through years 1 and 2. Exhibit 4 shows the industry-adjusted return on assets across upsizing and downsizing categories, relative to that of Stable Employers, from the year prior to the announcement (the base year) through the year of the announcement (year 0) and the subsequent two years. Note that for the sake of clarity, Exhibit 4 does not include results for the Combination Downsizers and Upsizers.

EXHIBIT 3 Change in Employment 1982–2000 (percent) by Employment-Change Category

Employment-Asset-Change Category	Year 0	Year 1	Year 2
Employment Downsizers (*n* = 657, 10.24% of total sample)	−10.87	1.83	3.38
Combination Downsizers (*n* = 224, 3.49%)	−20.30	1.67	2.92
Asset Downsizers (*n* = 93, 1.45%)	−16.86	5.16	7.75
Stable Employers (*n* = 2,770, 43.13 percent)	0.27	3.97	4.23
Asset Upsizers (*n* = 1,094, 17.03 percent)	28.08	22.49	20.10
Combination Upsizers (*n* = 1,172, 18.25 percent)	32.35	17.31	16.26
Employment Upsizers (*n* = 409, 6.37 percent)	13.98	10.71	11.46

Note: *n* refers to the number of occurrences in each category. Entries in each column under years 0, 1, and 2 are average results for each category.

As in our earlier study, notice how Downsizers, either Employment Downsizers or Asset Downsizers, never outperform Stable Employers in terms of industry-adjusted profitability (ROA).

STOCK RETURN

The final judgment as to the effectiveness of a management action is whether it can generate stock returns that are attractive to investors. Exhibit 5 shows the cumulative, industry-adjusted return from investing in a portfolio of companies in each category, starting at the

EXHIBIT 4 Industry-Adjusted Return on Assets, 1982–2000

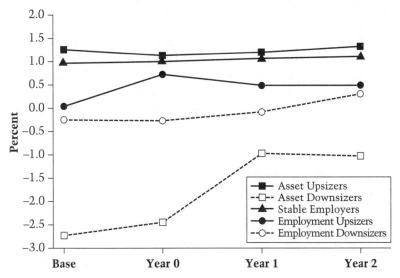

EXHIBIT 5 Return on Common Stock, Cumulative from Beginning of Event Year, 1982–2000

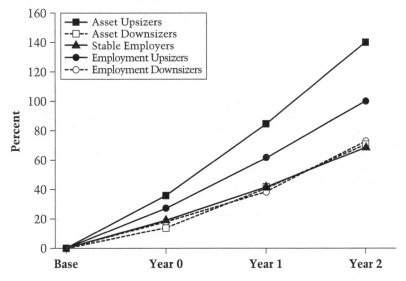

beginning of the year of the employment/asset change and continuing on through the following two years. These data represent the time period from 1982 through 2000.

What is the total compound return that an investor would have earned by the end of year 2 from an investment at the start of year 0 in a portfolio of companies in each category that earned the annual returns shown for years 0, 1, and 2? For each $1.00 invested, the investor would have the following by the end of year 2:

Stable Employers	$1.69
Employment Downsizers	$1.72
Asset Downsizers	$1.72
Employment Upsizers	$1.99
Asset Upsizers	$2.42

Exhibit 6 shows that the Asset Upsizers generated cumulative stock returns that were significantly higher than those of their industries—an average of 18 cents higher by the end of year 2. No other employment/asset change category would have generated returns that were significantly higher than those of their industries.

These results suggest that downsizing strategies, either employment downsizing or asset downsizing, do not yield long-term payoffs that are significantly larger than those generated by Stable Employers. The latter group includes those companies in which the complement of employees did not fluctuate by more than ±5 percent. This conclusion differs from that in our earlier analysis of the data from 1982 to 1994.[7] In that study, we concluded that some types of downsizing—namely, asset downsizing—do yield higher ROAs than either Stable Employers or their industries. However, when the data from 1995–2000 are added to the original 1982–1994 data, a different picture emerges. That picture suggests clearly that, at least during the time period of our study, it was not possible for firms to "save" or "shrink" their way to prosperity. Rather, it was only by growing their businesses (asset upsizing) that firms outperformed Stable Employers as well as their own industries in terms of profitability and total returns on common stock.

In pondering these results, it is important to keep in mind two limitations of the study. First, we were not able to adjust statistically for the state of each organization's financial health or for its industry's economic conditions prior to the changes in employment or assets. That is, while we did not look at what caused the

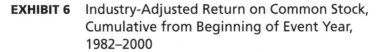

EXHIBIT 6 Industry-Adjusted Return on Common Stock, Cumulative from Beginning of Event Year, 1982–2000

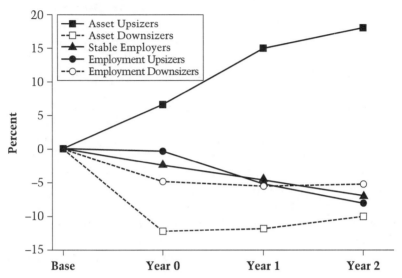

change, declining sales or profitability are factored into our results because we considered the *change* in profitability from year 0 to year 1 to year 2. Industry-adjusted returns also take into account the fact that all firms in an industry face the same set of economic conditions.

Second, we only looked at the specific reduction of expenses due to people. Surely a company facing declining sales must reduce expenses in order to avoid an even greater decline in profits. We did not look at other possible avenues of expense reduction. What our results show, however, is that reducing labor costs per se does not necessarily return a company to profitability.

Is It Always a Mistake to Downsize Employees?

Our results do not suggest that firms should not reduce the size of their workforces under any circumstances. In fact, many firms have downsized and restructured successfully to improve their productivity. General Electric under Jack Welch is a prime example.[8]

In the aggregate, the productivity and competitiveness of businesses in many different industries have increased in recent years. However, the lesson from our analysis is that firms cannot simply *assume* that layoffs are a quick fix that will necessarily lead to productivity improvements and increased financial performance. Increasing the likelihood that employment downsizings will result in the desired improvements requires a careful analysis of the expected consequences on all of a firm's stakeholders, including customers and local communities.

Managers of publicly owned firms have an obligation to run them as efficiently as possible. Even if these firms are large and stable, managers should be searching for ways to improve their firms' profitability, including adjusting their workforces. Yet, what is striking about the results of the employment downsizings is the negligible impact on firm profitability relative to the size of the layoffs. The Employment Downsizers reduced their work forces by an average of 10.87 percent in the year of the announcement and 5.66 percent by the end of year 2. While they did increase their returns on assets (ROAs) slightly (0.5 percent), their profitability never exceeded that of Stable Employers that did not downsize. Relative to their industries, they were able to attain a ROA that was only 0.3 percent above their industry average by the end of year 2. The Combination Downsizers reduced their workforces even more—20.3 percent in the year of the announcement and 15.71 percent by the end of year 2—yet showed profitability results that were little better than those of the Employment Downsizers.

What are the implications of this study? Senior managers are under considerable pressure from their stockholders to improve financial performance. Often they try to do this by cutting costs or restructuring assets. Many managers have accepted employment downsizing as a strategy for cutting costs in a manner that is tangible and predictable. Does such cost cutting translate into higher profits? Our research, done at the firm level rather than at the level of the strategic business unit, has not produced evidence that downsizing firms were able generally and significantly to improve profits or cumulative returns on common stock. On the other hand, the evidence indicates that upsizing firms were able to please their stockholders, and Asset Upsizers generated stock returns that were superior to those of their industries in every year after the base year.

Given these results, we conclude that employment downsizing may not generate the benefits sought by management. Managers must be very cautious in implementing a strategy that can impose such traumatic costs on employees, both on those who leave as well as on those who stay.[9] Management needs to be sure about the sources of future savings and carefully weigh those against *all* of the costs, including the increased costs associated with subsequent employment expansions, when economic conditions improve.

EMPLOYMENT DOWNSIZING AND FLEXIBILITY

This study did not directly address the issue of flexibility. However, many firms may have increased their strategic flexibility by thoughtful downsizing and asset restructuring. Certainly they sharpened the focus of their businesses by divesting business units that did not fit with their missions. Others eliminated excess employees and cut costs to improve their competitiveness.

However, there is a paradox in the attempt to make a company "lean and mean," while maintaining the flexibility to "turn on a dime." To turn on a dime, a company must have the flexibility to take advantage of emerging prospects. To a great extent, flexibility depends on the firm having some excess capacity, or slack. For example, to increase production when demand increases, a manufacturing firm needs to have some excess production capacity in its plants; and, to take advantage of new investment opportunities, a firm needs unused financial resources. This need for excess capacity applies at least as much to its people as it does to its physical plant or its financial resources. Even if the firm has the physical and financial resources, its ability to make productive use of those resources will be constrained by its human resources. Simply put, it needs people to implement its plans, expansions, and investments, particularly in the increasingly service and information-dominated economies around the world. Consequently, it may be advantageous to maintain human resources even in slower periods to support flexibility. We will have more to say about the virtues of employment stability in chapter 6.

3

A Baker's Dozen Myths versus Facts about Downsizing

When confronted with the need to reduce costs, many of the same executives who tout people as "our greatest asset" see those assets as ripe opportunities for cutting costs.

MYTH #1 ▪ **Jobs are secure at firms that are doing well financially.**

FACT ▪ **Preemptive layoffs by large firms are common.**
Today's job cuts are not solely about large, sick companies trying to save themselves, as was often the case in the early 1990s (e.g., IBM, Sears). They are also about healthy companies hoping to reduce costs and boost earnings by reducing head count (e.g., Goldman Sachs, AOL). They are about trying to preempt tough times instead of simply reacting to them. These layoffs are radical, preventive first aid.[1] On the other hand, small companies, especially small manufacturers, tend to resist layoffs because they are trying to protect the substantial investments they made in finding and training workers.[2]

MYTH #2 ▪ **Companies that are laying off workers are not hiring new ones.**

FACT ■ **Companies are tailoring their complements of skills.**
When it comes to layoffs, appearances can be deceiving. At the same time as firms are firing some people, they are hiring others, presumably people with the skills to execute new strategies. Wal-mart.com laid off more than 20 employees at its online enterprise in early 2001, but it subsequently added as many new hires and even grew by more than 25 percent. Hewlett-Packard shed some marketing jobs while adding new positions in sales and consulting. Fully one-third of businesses that downsized since 1994 wound up restoring some of the eliminated positions, and nearly 50 percent created positions to meet emerging needs, according to a recent study by career services firm Lee Hecht Harrison.[3]

According to the American Management Association's year 2000 survey of its member companies, companies that employ one-quarter of the American workforce, 36 percent of firms that eliminated jobs in the previous 12 months said they had also created new positions. That's up from 31 percent in 1996.[4] The Society for Human Resource Management found similar results in a 2001 survey.[5] As companies lose workers in one department, they are adding people with different skills in another, continually tailoring their workforces to fit the available work and adjusting quickly to swings in demand for products and services. What makes this flexibility possible is the rise of temporary and contract workers. On a typical day they allow companies to meet 12 percent of their staffing needs. On peak days that figure may reach 20 percent.[6]

MYTH #3 ■ **Downsizing employees boosts profits.**

FACT ■ **Profitability does not necessarily follow downsizing.**
Data presented in chapter 2 from the S&P 500, 1982–2000, showed clearly that profitability, as measured by the return on assets, does not necessarily follow downsizing, even as long as two years later.[7] Survey data support this conclusion. Thus, the *2001 Layoffs and Job Security Survey*, conducted by the Society for Human Resource Management, reported that only 32 percent of respondents indicated that layoffs improved profits.[8] Even massive staff cutbacks at firms such as Eastman Kodak, Apple Computer, and AT&T have not produced increased earnings years later.[9]

MYTH #4 ▪ **Downsizing employees boosts productivity.**

FACT ▪ **Productivity results after downsizing are mixed.**
The American Management Association surveyed 700 companies
that had downsized in the 1990s. In 34 percent of the cases, productivity rose, but it fell in 30 percent of them.[10] These results are
consistent with those reported in another study of 250,000 manufacturing plants by the National Bureau of Economic Research.
That study concluded that the productivity-enhancing role of employment downsizing has been exaggerated. While some plants did
downsize and post healthy gains in productivity, even more (including many of the largest facilities) managed to raise output per
worker while expanding employment. They contributed about as
much to overall productivity increases in manufacturing as did the
successful downsizers.[11]

MYTH #5 ▪ **Downsizing employees has no effect on the
quality of products or services.**

FACT ▪ **For most employers, downsizing employees does
not lead to long-term improvements in the quality of
products or services.**
Chapter 1 described the tragic results of poor labor relations on
product quality in one tire-manufacturing plant at Bridgestone/
Firestone. However, that example alone does not address the question "Does employment downsizing per se affect product quality?"
In its 1996 survey on corporate downsizing, job elimination, and
job creation, the American Management Association reported that
over the long term, only 35 percent of responding companies increased the quality of their products and services after laying off
employees. However, among those that did increase quality, 74
percent also increased profits.[12] While there is a strong relationship between improvements in the quality of products and services and increases in profits, downsizing the workforce is not the
way to get there.

MYTH #6 ▪ **Downsizing employees is a one-time event for
most companies.**

FACT ▪ **The best predictor of whether a company will
downsize in a given year is whether it has downsized the
previous year.**

One of the clearest trends is that downsizing begets more downsizing, as ongoing staff reductions are etched into the corporate culture. On average two-thirds of firms that lay off employees in a given year do so again the following year.[13] Among companies that laid off employees since 2000, according to the *2001 Layoffs and Job Security Survey*, 45 percent rehired laid-off employees full time, and 17 percent rehired laid-off employees as consultants. Fully 56 percent have hired new employees since the layoff.[14]

MYTH #7 ▪ Since companies are just "cutting fat" by downsizing employees, there are no adverse effects on those who remain.

FACT ▪ For the majority of companies, downsizing has had adverse effects on the morale, workload, and commitment of "survivors."

It has often been said that employee morale is the first casualty in a downsizing. Survey data bear this out. Right Associates found that 70 percent of senior managers who remained in downsized firms reported that morale and trust declined. Study after study has found similar results.[15] A recent national survey found the following among survivors: feel overworked (54 percent), are overwhelmed by workload (55 percent), lack time for reflection (59 percent), don't have time to complete tasks (56 percent), and have to multitask too much (45 percent).[16]

Between 1993 and 1995, an Australian bank, identified simply as Onebank, implemented a "restructuring improvement program" (yielding the ominous acronym RIP). Its objective was to improve the bank's competitiveness by reducing costs, instigating a sales culture, and installing new technology. RIP eliminated 350 branches and 10,000 employees, although 4,500 new jobs were created in the central processing sites. RIP involved a "spill and fill" process in which all staff lost their jobs and had to compete for the jobs remaining in the new structure. It was like a giant game of musical chairs, with about 20 percent fewer chairs than people.

An academic's survey of the bank's middle managers (to which a remarkable 80 percent responded) revealed an almost complete turnaround in attitudes toward their careers. The survey found a decline in the managers' commitment at all levels: to their job, to their branch or department, and, most of all, to Onebank and its goals. This was true even though 83 percent considered RIP essential for the long-term future of the bank, and 76 percent said they were fully committed to making it a success.

How had the restructuring changed the nature of the managers' jobs? More than 30 percent of the managers said they now had more staff reporting to them, 64 percent had increased responsibility, 69 percent had a wider range of duties, 77 percent worked longer hours, 83 percent experienced increased stress, and 85 percent had an increased workload overall.

Against all that, however, only 37 percent said they'd received a salary increase. Is it any surprise that 49 percent felt a decreased sense of commitment to Onebank or that 64 percent experienced decreased job satisfaction? Asked about their level of commitment and their views on working for the bank, the managers offered 8 positive and 390 negative comments.[17]

MYTH #8 ▪ **Most employees are surprised to learn they've been laid off. They ask, "Why me?"**

FACT ▪ **Downsized employees often express sympathy toward an employer's reasons for layoffs, and many refuse to personalize the experience.**
From the perspective of employees, layoffs have a new character. More managers are briefing employees regularly about the economic status of their companies. This raises their awareness and actually prepares employees for what might happen to them. To many, the layoffs seem justified because of the slowdown in economic growth, the plunge in corporate profits, and the dive in stock prices. While it used to be (and still is) traumatic to be laid off even once, some employees can now expect to go through that experience twice or even three times before they reach 50.[18]

MYTH #9 ▪ **At outplacement centers, laid-off employees tend to keep to themselves as they pursue jobs.**

FACT ▪ **Outplacement centers have become America's new hiring halls—gathering places for those between assignments.**
There seems to be a new matter-of-factness about downsizing. As the managing principal of the New York office of outplacement firm Right Associates put it, "These people are not ashamed, but they do feel dislocated, and there is anger. They were on track and

now they are trying to get back on track." Right has redesigned its offices to accommodate this new trend. Instead of enclosed offices and cubicles, where the downsized of the 1990s kept to themselves as they pursued jobs, there are many more glass walls and open gathering places where the downsized of the 21st century get to know each other. They socialize, and they even re-create office buzz. Said the managing principal, "It took us a while to recognize this had become important."

MYTH #10 ■ **The number of employees let go, including their associated costs, is the total cost of downsizing.**

FACT ■ **In knowledge-based or relationship-based businesses, the most serious cost is the loss of employee contacts, business foregone, and lack of innovation.**

In knowledge- and relationship-based businesses, the company's most important assets walk out the door every night. *The Economist* magazine noted that people are not interchangeable. They all have different skills and add value in different ways. "Downsizing can have a devastating impact on innovation, as skills and contacts that have been developed over the years are destroyed at a stroke."[19]

Knowledge-based businesses, from high-technology firms to the financial services industry, depend heavily on their employees—their stock of human capital—to innovate and grow. They are "learning organizations"—collections of networks in which interrelationships among individuals (i.e., social networks) generate learning and knowledge. This knowledge base constitutes a firm's "memory." Downsizing is especially hazardous to learning organizations. Because a single individual has multiple relationships in such an organization, indiscriminate, nonselective downsizing has the potential to inflict considerable damage on the learning and memory capacity of organizations.[20] That damage is far greater than might be implied by a simple tally of the number of individuals let go.

When one considers the multiple relationships generated by one individual, it is clear that restructuring that involves significant reductions in employees can inflict damage and create the loss of significant "chunks" of organizational memory. Such a loss damages ongoing processes and operations, forfeits current contacts, and may lead to foregone business opportunities. Which kinds of organizations are at greatest risk? Those that operate in rapidly evolving industries, such as biotechnology, pharmaceuticals, and software, in which survival depends on a firm's ability to innovate constantly.

MYTH #11 ▪ Violence, sabotage, or other vengeful acts from laid-off employees are remote possibilities.

FACT ▪ They are less remote than you think, and the consequences may be severe.

The good news is that the *2001 Layoffs and Job Security Survey*, conducted by the Society for Human Resource Management, reported that 86 percent of companies have not experienced discrimination charges, and 93 percent have not experienced workplace violence. The bad news, however, is that the most common precipitator of workplace violence is a layoff or firing.[21]

What do Xerox, Fireman's Fund, and the U.S. Postal Service have in common? They have employees who died violently while at work. Violence disrupts productivity, causes untold damage to those exposed to the trauma, is related to workplace abuse of drugs or alcohol and absenteeism, and costs employers millions of dollars.[22] In a stressed-out, downsized business environment, people are searching for someone to blame for their problems. With the loss of a job or other event the employee perceives as unfair, the employer may become the focus of a disgruntled individual's fear and frustration. Under these circumstances, some form of workplace aggression—that is, efforts by individuals to harm others with whom they work, or have worked, or their organization itself—is likely.[23]

In France, laid-off workers at bankrupt household appliance maker Moulinex SA threatened to blow up their factory if their demands for more severance pay were not met. A sign in black marker at the entrance to the plant said it all: "Money or BOOM!" Their demands were met. The French labor ministry and the unions agreed on a deal to give workers who were with Moulinex for more than 25 years a severance bonus of 12,200 euros (about $10,785) and the rest of the workers 4,600 to 7,600 euros (about $4,050 to $6,690).[24]

Among white-collar workers, the cyber saboteur has emerged as a new threat among disgruntled ex-employees. Recently axed workers have posted a company's payroll on its intranet, planted data-destroying bugs, and handed over valuable intellectual property to competitors. Although exact numbers are hard to come by, computer security experts say it is fast becoming the top technical concern at many companies.

Of course, fired workers have exacted revenge on their former employers in the past. But this time, they're capable of great damage, because more than ever, companies depend on computer networks that are vulnerable to electronic sabotage. With more than 30,000 Web sites filled with hacking tools that any grade-school child could use, today's brand of getting even is far easier for alienated workers to pull off. It's also far more costly for companies. The FBI estimates the cost of the average insider attack at $2.7 million.[25]

MYTH #12 ▪ Training survivors during and following layoffs is not necessary.

FACT ▪ Training survivors is critical to success subsequently.

The American Management Association survey on corporate downsizing, job elimination, and job creation clearly supports this conclusion. In firms in which training budgets increased after downsizing, 63 percent reported that productivity increased over the long term, and 69 percent reported that profits increased. In firms in which training budgets decreased after downsizing, only 34 percent reported that productivity increased over the long term, and only 40 percent reported that profits increased. A similar pattern also emerged over the short term.

One explanation for these results is that two-thirds of reported job eliminations are connected to organizational restructuring or business process reengineering. Workers who receive training are far more likely to improve their productivity, which, in turn, leads to increases in profits.[26]

MYTH #13 ▪ Stress-related medical disorders are more likely for those laid off than for those who remain.

FACT ▪ Workers at downsized companies are just as likely to suffer adverse health consequences.

Among employees who remain after a downsizing, more than half report increased job stress and symptoms of "burnout." The physical toll on workers translates into a financial toll on employers.

Based on an analysis of 3,896 disability cases, Northwestern National Life Insurance Company calculated that the average cost of rehabilitating an employee disabled because of stress was $1,925 ($2,850 in 2001 dollars). If he or she is not rehabilitated, companies will need to hold in reserve an average of $73,270 ($108,450 in 2001 dollars) or more to cover payments for employees disabled by job-related stress.[27]

Another study of 300 large and midsize firms was conducted jointly by Cigna Insurance Company and the American Management Association. Over the five-year period of the study, stress-related disorders among workers at downsizing companies showed the greatest increase among all kinds of medical-related claims, including those for mental health and substance abuse, high blood pressure, and other cardiovascular problems. The percentage increases across companies varied from 100 to 900 percent— that is, as much as a ninefold increase. The same survey revealed that although supervisors comprise 5 to 8 percent of the American workforce, this group is at a greater risk of being laid off and of developing a stress-related disability.[28]

While research has revealed a variety of negative health consequences associated with layoff victims,[29] this is not necessarily true for those who accept voluntary buyout packages. In a recent Australian study, 71 individuals who had accepted voluntary buyout packages (after 7 to 44 years of service, with an average of 25 years) were contacted 2 to 7 years after leaving their firms. Almost 90 percent were married, and about half had dependent children. Surprisingly, 61 percent considered their health to be about the same, and 29 percent considered it to be "better" or "much better."[30]

Other research has shown that one's financial situation is a major factor in how people perceive and respond to job loss, both physiologically and psychologically.[31] Financial incentives, which often accompany voluntary severance agreements, may well moderate the ill effects of job loss. As one set of authors noted, "evidence is mounting that events viewed as uncontrollable and undesirable are more likely to be associated with psychological and physical distress."[32] The findings of this study suggest that rather than considering themselves as "victims," individuals who are offered voluntary buyouts may see themselves as having the opportunity to make choices about their future prospects that are not available to the "survivors."[33] As a result, they experience less distress later on.

4

The Case for Responsible Restructuring

Instead of asking, "What's the irreducible core number of people we need to run our business?" responsible restructuring asks, "How can we change the way we do business, so that we can use the people we currently have most effectively?"

As we saw in chapter 2, a pure employment downsizing approach, which changes the number of people without changing the way work is done, generally does not produce the long-term effects its proponents had hoped for. In contrast, many companies are "responsibly restructuring"—relying on their workers to provide sustained competitive advantage and adopting a wide range of practices, such as these:

- Skills training and continuous learning
- Information sharing
- Employee participation in the design and implementation of work processes
- Flattened organizational structures
- Labor–management partnerships
- Compensation linked to employee skills and organizational performance
- Customer satisfaction—as defined by customers

Research has quantified the relationship between practices like these and performance improvement, including longer-term financial performance. The evidence indicates that such practices are usually associated with increases in productivity (defined as output per worker), as well as with a firm's long-term financial performance.[1] However, these effects are most pronounced when such work practices are implemented together as a system.[2] The study to be described next examined four alternative approaches to the employment relationship to determine whether investments in employees pay off.

ALTERNATIVE APPROACHES TO THE EMPLOYMENT RELATIONSHIP

Consider four basic approaches that an employer might use to relate to employees:[3]

- Quasi–spot contract
- Mutual investment
- Underinvestment
- Overinvestment

A *quasi–spot contract* relationship resembles a pure economic exchange, for it is purely transactional. The employer offers short-term, purely economic inducements in exchange for well-specified contributions by the employee. A classic example is that between a brokerage firm and a stockbroker. The employer–employee relationship is defined in terms of specified activities for a set compensation. Neither party expects anything more, nor does either party have an obligation to maintain a long-term relationship.

In contrast, a *mutual investment* employee–organization relationship exists when the employer offers something more than short-term monetary rewards. It offers extended consideration of an employee's well-being, as well as investments in the employee's career within the firm. In exchange, the employee agrees to work on job assignments that fall outside prior agreements or expertise, to assist junior colleagues, to accept job transfers when requested by the employer to do so, and to learn firm-specific skills that are not readily transferable to other employers. The employee trusts that such investments will be reciprocated over the long term.

Conversely, an *underinvestment* relationship exists when the employee is expected to undertake broad and open-ended obligations while the employer reciprocates with short-term, specified monetary rewards, with no commitment to a long-term relationship or investment in the employee's training or career. This type of relationship is typical of many employers in competitive industries because they desire full commitment from employees yet at the same time want the flexibility to lay off employees virtually at will. This approach is more favorable to employers than to employees.

A fourth type of employment relationship, *overinvestment*, is more favorable to employees. Employees in organizations bound by trade union contracts, and some government bureaucracies, are managed by this approach. That is, the employee performs only a well-specified set of job-focused activities, but the employer offers open-ended and broad-ranging rewards, including training and a commitment to provide the employee with career opportunities. Employees in these organizations enjoy relatively high employment security and have received considerable training investments from their employers without necessarily being expected to make contributions that go beyond their immediate jobs.

WHICH APPROACHES PRODUCE BETTER OUTCOMES?

Comparisons among the four approaches were based on survey responses, plus supervisory and peer ratings of performance, from 976 employees and 205 supervisors across 10 different organizations in 5 different competitive industries. There was general support for the mutual investment employee–organization relationship. In this approach, open-ended inducements provided by employers are balanced by open-ended contributions from employees. Employees working under these arrangements generally performed better, as rated both by supervisors and by peers, and had more favorable attitudes than employees managed under any of the other three arrangements. They were more committed to their jobs and organizations; they endorsed the overall fairness of decisions regarding pay, promotions, and performance reviews; and they believed that their coworkers could be relied on and had integrity. The mutual-investment employee–organization relationship is similar to what have been termed "high-involvement," "high-commitment," or "high-performance" work practices.[4]

The overinvestment approach, in which the employee performs only a well-specified set of job-focused activities, while the employer offers open-ended and broad-ranging rewards, also was associated with higher levels of performance and more favorable attitudes than either the underinvestment or quasi–spot contract approach. However, the mutual-investment approach resulted in better performance and more favorable employee attitudes than any of the other approaches.

The underinvestment approach produced the worst results on both employee performance and attitudes. Employees managed under this arrangement reacted by reducing their performance on core tasks, as they refrained from doing anything beyond their core tasks, and by being absent more often.

Results also suggested that in adopting an underinvestment or quasi–spot contract approach, employers may sacrifice employee performance. Although workforce reductions may lead to reduced labor costs, decreased employee performance and commitment under these employment approaches may have a negative effect on firms in the long run.

Alternatively, employees seem to respond favorably both in terms of their performance and their attitudes when employers are willing to commit to fairly long-term relationships with them and to provide some degree of employment security. In short, the employment flexibility of the underinvestment and quasi–spot contract approaches may involve a trade-off—reduced performance from employees.[5] The lesson from these results is clear: There is a payoff from treating your employees as assets to be developed, rather than as costs to be cut.

THE CAUSAL EFFECT OF MANAGEMENT PRACTICES ON PERFORMANCE

Further evidence that management practices affect performance comes from studies in the automobile industry and from the survival rate of newly public companies.

- Automobile plants with innovative work systems—such as extensive training, performance-based compensation, work teams, and reassignment of quality control responsibility to line workers—manufactured vehicles in an average of 22 hours with 0.5 defect per vehicle. In contrast, more traditional plants that used similar technology took 30 hours with 0.8 defect per vehicle.[6]

■ Another study examined the five-year survival rate of 136 nonfinancial companies that initiated their public offerings in the U.S. stock market in 1988.[7] By 1993, some five years later, only 60 percent of these companies were still in existence. The researchers controlled statistically for factors such as size, industry, and even profits. Results showed that both the value the firm placed on human resources— such as whether the company cited employees as a source of competitive advantage—and how the organization rewarded people—such as stock options for all employees and profit sharing—were significantly related to the likelihood of survival.

The results were important in a practical sense as well. In terms of the value they attached to people, firms that scored in the upper 16 percent of all firms in the sample were almost 20 percent more likely to survive than those that scored in the lower 16 percent of all firms in the sample. The difference in survival depending on where the firm scored on rewards to employees was even more dramatic, with a difference in five-year survival probability of 42 percent between firms in the upper and lower ends of the distribution. Overall, both the level of human resource value and the level of organization-based employee rewards (profit sharing, stock options for all employees) can greatly increase the likelihood of a firm's survival, although the effect of employee rewards is stronger.

As these examples show, adoption of so-called high-performance work practices that focus on developing and making the most effective use of an organization's human assets can have an economically significant effect on the market value of the firm. How large an effect? Recent work indicates a range of $15,000 to $45,000 per employee.[8] For example, one study examined the financial impact of human resource (HR) systems across 702 firms. An *HR system* refers to each firm's overall approach to managing people, comprising its activities related to staffing, retention, development, adjustment, and change management. Statistical analyses revealed that an improvement of one standard deviation in the HR system (movement from the 50th to the 84th percentile) was associated with an increase in shareholder wealth that averaged $41,000 per employee—about a 14 percent market value premium.[9] Hence, the use of progressive management practices benefits shareholders as well as employees.

THE FINANCIAL IMPACT OF EMPLOYEE ATTITUDES ON FIRM PERFORMANCE

Can the attitudes of employees affect a firm's performance in the market place? In fact, managers are interested in employees' attitudes, such as job satisfaction and commitment, principally because of the relationship between attitudes and behavior. They assume that employees who are dissatisfied with their jobs and who are not committed strongly to their organizations will tend to be absent or late for work, to quit more often, and to place less emphasis on customer satisfaction than those whose attitudes are positive. Poor job attitudes therefore lead to lowered productivity and organizational performance. Evidence indicates that this is, in fact, the case, and that management's concern is well placed.[10]

Sears, Roebuck & Co. studied the relationship between employee attitudes, customer behavior, and profits. In retailing, there is a chain of cause and effect running from employee behavior to customer behavior to profits. An employee's behavior, in turn, depends to a large extent on his or her attitude.

Over two quarters, Sears managers collected survey data from employees and customers and financial data from 800 of its stores. A team of consulting statisticians then factor-analyzed the data into meaningful clusters and assessed cause–effect relationships using statistical modeling techniques. Based on initial results, Sears adjusted the model and continued to collect data in order to apply it at the end of the next quarter.

How did Sears benefit from the model? It could see how employee attitudes drove not just customer service but also employee turnover and the likelihood that employees would recommend Sears and its merchandise to friends, family, and customers. It discovered that an employee's ability to see the connection between his or her work and the company's strategic objectives was a driver of positive behavior. It also found that asking customers whether Sears is a "fun place to shop" revealed more than a long list of more specific questions would. It began to see exactly how a change in training or business literacy affected revenues.

Although Sears used a 70-item questionnaire to assess employees' attitudes, it found that a mere 10 of those questions captured the predictive relationship among employee attitudes, behavior toward the customer, and customer satisfaction. Items such as the following predicted an employee's attitude about his or her job:

- I like the kind of work I do.
- I am proud to say I work at Sears.
- How does the way you are treated by those who supervise you influence your *overall attitude* about your job?

Items such as the following predicted an employee's attitude about the company:

- I feel good about the future of the company.
- I understand our business strategy.
- Do you see a connection between the work you do and the company's strategic objectives?

In summary, Sears produced a model, revised it three times, and created a kind of scorecard for the company—which it calls the Sears Total Performance Indicators, or TPI, that shows pathways of causation all the way from employee attitudes to profits. The company conducts interviews and collects data continually, assembles its information quarterly, and recalculates the impacts on its model annually to stay abreast of the changing economy, changing demographics, and changing competitive circumstances. The revised model helps Sears managers run the company.

For example, consider the quality of management as a driver of employee attitudes. The model shows that a 5-point improvement in employee attitudes will drive a 1.3-point improvement in customer satisfaction in the next quarter, which, in turn, will drive a 0.5 percent improvement in revenue growth. If Sears knew nothing about a local store except that employee attitudes had improved by 5 points on its survey instrument, it could predict with confidence that if revenue growth in the district as a whole were 5 percent, revenue growth at this particular store would be 5.5 percent. Every year an outside accounting firm audits these numbers as closely as it audits financial measures.

Impact on Managers' Behavior and on the Firm   In a revolutionary step, Sears now bases all long-term executive incentives on the TPI—that is, on nonfinancial as well as financial performance—one-third on employee measures, one-third on customer measures, and one-third on traditional investor measures. At the level of the firm, employee satisfaction on Sears's TPI rose 4 percent and customer satisfaction by almost 4 percent in one year. The 4 percent improvement translated into more than $200 million in additional revenues for that year. That increased Sears's market capitalization (price per share times the number of shares outstanding) by nearly $250 million.[11]

Now that we know that an employee's attitudes affect his or her behavior in front of a customer, which affects the customer's decision to recommend Sears to others and to return to shop at Sears, which affects revenue growth, a reasonable question is this. "What specific policies and practices lead to high performance?" Let's consider that question next.

POLICIES AND PRACTICES THAT LEAD TO HIGH PERFORMANCE

Since 1990, researchers Brian Becker and Mark Huselid have conducted biannual surveys of HR management systems in U.S. publicly held companies—those with sales exceeding $5 million and more than 100 employees. They then match the data on HR systems with publicly available data on financial performance. This ongoing research program includes more than 2,800 corporations. Each survey enables them to construct an index that measures the extent to which a firm's HR system is consistent with the principles of a high-performance HR strategy. Consider just a few of the differences between firms in the top and bottom of the HR index as shown on page 45:[12]

Note the striking differences between firms in the top and bottom of the HR index. Firms with high-performance work systems adopt practices that are very different from those with low-performance work systems. They devote considerably more

HR PRACTICES	BOTTOM 10%	TOP 10%
Number of qualified applicants per position	8.24	36.55
Percentage hired based on a validated selection test	4.26	29.67
Percentage of jobs filled from within	34.90	61.46
Hours of training for new employees (< 1 year)	35.02	116.87
Hours of training for experienced employees	13.40	72.00
Percentage of employees receiving a regular performance appraisal	41.31	95.17
Percentage of workforce whose merit pay increase or incentive is tied to performance	23.36	87.27
Percentage of workforce routinely working in a self-managed, cross-functional, or project team	10.64	42.28
FIRM PERFORMANCE		
Employee turnover	34.09	20.87
Sales per employee	$158,101	$617,576
Market value to book value	3.64	11.06

resources to recruiting and selection, they train with much greater vigor, they do a lot more performance management and tie compensation to it, and they use teams to a much greater extent. As Becker and Huselid note, "Indeed, the most striking attribute of these comparisons is not any one HR management practice—it is not recruiting or training or compensation. Rather, the differences are much more comprehensive—and systemic."[13]

Note also that firms with the most effective HR management systems exhibited dramatically higher performance than those with the least effective HR management systems. Employee turnover was close to half, sales per employee were four times as great, and the ratio of the firm's market value to the book value of its assets was more than three times as large in high-performing companies. The ratio of market to book value is a key indicator of management's quality, for it demonstrates the extent to which management has increased shareholders' initial investment.

The extent to which high-performance work practices actually will pay off depends on the skill and care with which they are implemented to solve real business problems and to support a firm's operating and strategic initiatives. Firms that restructure by implementing high-performance work practices are committed to making progress *together* with their workers, rather than *at the expense of* their workers.

Organizations get a workforce that makes them more competitive, while employees get more interesting, satisfying jobs, together with the income that will support a middle-class lifestyle. In an era when job security is but a fond memory, responsible restructuring offers the promise of sustained profitability for businesses and a rising standard of living for employees. To put restructuring efforts into broader perspective, let us consider the true driver of business success in the new millennium: business concept innovation.

BUSINESS CONCEPT INNOVATION

As Gary Hamel notes in his book *Leading the Revolution*,[14] the age of incremental progress is over. Its mantra—faster, better, cheaper—is true of fewer and fewer companies. Today change has changed. No longer is it additive. No longer does it move in a straight line (linear). It is now discontinuous, abrupt, and distinctly nonlinear. Perhaps the most far-reaching change of all is the Internet, for the Internet has rendered geography meaningless.

In the age of incremental progress, companies practiced rigorous planning, continuous improvement, statistical process control (SPC), six sigma, reengineering, and enterprise requirements planning (ERP). If companies missed something that was changing in the environment, for example, in TVs, stereos, and other consumer electronics, as in the 1970s and 1980s, there was plenty of time to catch up.

Today, if a company misses a critical new development—for example, in digital phones, Internet auctions, or corporate extranets— it may never catch up. As an example of the latter, consider ERP. Firms employed lots of consultants to help them use ERP to integrate internal operations such as purchasing, manufacturing, and accounting. This is important and useful to do, but now companies use the Web to link up with suppliers and customers.

Many ERP consultants (and their firms) are not players in this area, and the Web will be used in ever more innovative ways in the future.

Industrial age management is a liability in a postindustrial world. Never before has there been such an incredible need for visionary leadership and the capacity to manage change effectively. Today the challenge is to think differently—to move beyond scientific management and kaizen (small improvements in efficiency each year). As Hamel points out, the focus today is not on the slow accretion of scientific knowledge but on leaps of human imagination. In a nonlinear world, only nonlinear ideas will create new wealth and lead to radical improvements in human welfare.

In introducing its list of the global most admired companies, *Fortune* had this to say about business concept innovation:

> When he chose the phrase "only the paranoid survive" for the title of his autobiography, Intel Chairman Andy Grove was referring to the frenzied pace of the new economy, a place where dramatic innovations can transform an entire industry in less time than it takes Tiger Woods to break par. Even companies that successfully juggle the competing demands of customers, employees, and shareholders can suddenly find themselves on the brink of obsolescence, their products and services supplanted by the Next Big Thing. Those who reach the top of *Fortune*'s annual list of the "World's Most Admired Companies" adhere to Grove's dictum. And the key to staying ahead of the pack is constant innovation.[15]

Now let's consider what business concept innovation is not.

WHAT BUSINESS CONCEPT INNOVATION IS NOT

Some popular strategies today are spin-offs of noncore businesses, stock buy-backs, tracking stocks, and efficiency programs. All of these *release* wealth, but they do not *create* wealth.[16] This is financial engineering, not business concept innovation. Strategies like these do not create new customers, new markets, or new streams of revenues. Their only purpose is to wring a bit more wealth out of yesterday's strategies. Sure, money talks, but it doesn't think. Machines work efficiently, but they don't invent.[17] Thinking and inventing are done by the only true, long-term source of innovation and renewal that organizations possess—smart, well-trained people.

How do you increase the probability that radical, new, wealth-creating ideas will emerge in your organization? Certainly not by indiscriminate downsizing of your workforce or by trying to imitate the best practices of other companies. Rather, a key task for leaders is to create an environment in which the creativity and imagination of employees at *all* levels can flourish. In many cases doing so requires a radical shift in the mind-set of managers at all levels. That new mind-set is called *responsible restructuring*, and in our next chapter we will present examples of firms that are implementing it.

5

Responsible Restructuring— Alternative Strategies

Many companies, when faced with competitive pressures, have found creative alternatives to downsizing their workforces.

CHARLES SCHWAB & COMPANY

Strategy: Use downsizing as a last resort; at the same time, reinvent your business.

At the end of the second quarter of 2001, Schwab's commission revenues were off 57 percent from their peak 15 months earlier. Overall revenue was down 38 percent, losses totaled $19 million (U.S.), and the stock had dropped 75 percent from its high. Something had to be done. How did the company respond? It took five steps before finally cutting staff.[1]

- When Schwab saw business begin to deteriorate the year before, it put projects on hold and cut back on such expenses as catered staff lunches and travel and entertainment. Management went out of its way to explain to employees the short-term nature of these cuts.[2]

- As it became clear that more savings were needed, top executives all took pay cuts: 50 percent each for the company's two CEOs, 20 percent for executive vice presidents, 10 percent for senior vice presidents, and 5 percent for vice presidents.

- It encouraged employees to take unused vacation and to take unpaid leaves of up to 20 days.
- Management designated certain Fridays as voluntary days off without pay for employees who didn't have clients to deal with.
- Only after the outlook darkened again, at the end of the first quarter of 2001, did the firm announce layoffs—2,000 out of a workforce of 25,000. Even then the severance package included a $7,500 "hire-back" bonus that any employee will get if he or she is rehired within 18 months. It also included between 500 and 1,000 stock options, cash payments to offset the increased costs of health-care insurance for laid-off employees, and a full range of outplacement services.[3] Furthermore, everyone being laid off, nearly 5,000 people by the end of September 2001, is eligible for a $20,000 tuition voucher paid for by the founder himself. That could cost him as much as $10 million.

Over the past decade or so, Schwab has a lengthy record of product innovation. Perhaps its greatest innovation appeared to be one of the gutsiest moves of the 1990s—offering online trading in a bigger and better way than anyone else, even though it meant cutting commission rates by more than half. The result? In early 2000 Schwab could boast of having generated a better 10-year return for investors than Microsoft!

Today, however, the company is reinventing its business model. Sure, it is cutting costs by making its Web site easier to use, thus cutting down on expensive phone traffic, and it is raising fees for customers who don't trade very often and are unprofitable for the firm. But its biggest bet—where it thinks the bulk of its future revenue will come from—will be a radical new approach to winning and keeping business. The firm that was founded on the principle that it would never tell customers what stocks to buy is about to do just that, but with an ingenious twist.

The plan is to have computers analyze customers' portfolios, compare them with a computer-generated list of Schwab-recommended stocks for that investor's risk profile, and then convey that message to the client. When the objective analysis is supplemented with research reports from partner Goldman Sachs, plus occasional access to a salaried investment specialist, the company feels this will fill in the final gap in what will be a complete set of services for virtually every investor.

Schwab is practicing responsible restructuring. Why? Because at the same time that it is demonstrating by its actions that it sees its employees as assets to be developed, it is developing business concept innovations that will allow it to generate new customers and new streams of revenue in order to grow its business. A second strategy is to focus on meeting the needs of survivors. Compaq Computer illustrates that approach.

COMPAQ COMPUTER

Strategy: Do everything you can to manage survivors well.

In the early 1990s, long before Compaq Computer laid off 15 percent of its workforce to compete more effectively with companies having lower-cost products on the market, it developed a campaign to communicate information about the layoff. It reasoned that if survivors understood fully the strategic reasons for the downsizing, negative rumors would be less likely because employees would know where Compaq was heading and what steps were necessary for the company to achieve its objectives.[4]

Line managers were responsible for communicating information about the layoffs to their employees. The managers were a credible source of information, and they could answer questions immediately. Prior to the downsizing, the managers went through a training program that had two objectives: learn how to provide support to the victims and help to surviving employees. During a four-hour training session, the managers received up-to-date information about the competitive environment for PCs, the reasons for the layoffs, and demonstrations on how to conduct meetings with their subordinates to explain the company's strategic moves to them. The managers also received a list of potential questions from subordinates and suggestions on how to answer them.

Compaq went out of its way to tell survivors how the departing employees were being treated and what the company was doing for them. It reasoned that survivors would view the entire restructuring process more positively if they knew their departing colleagues were being treated fairly and with dignity.

These communication efforts worked. Employees accepted the downsizing as inevitable and necessary for Compaq's survival, and they continued to innovate. Eight months later, the company introduced a full range of lower-cost products—which was the driving force behind the layoffs in the first place. Three years later, sales had almost tripled over their prelayoff level, and there were no further layoffs in the interim.

Now fast-forward to late 2001. The PC industry was dealing with its worst-ever downturn that had resulted in $1.2 billion in losses and 31,000 layoffs industry-wide.[5] To survive and grow, Compaq announced a deal to be acquired by Hewlett-Packard in mid-2002. The new behemoth is projected to have a 19 percent market share and $87 billion of revenues. The combined company also projects savings of $2.5 billion a year by 2004, largely by cutting 15,000 jobs and eliminating duplication. After an affirmative proxy vote and dismissal by a Delaware court of a lawsuit challenging the deal, it appears that Hewlett-Packard's acquisition of Compaq will proceed. It will be interesting to see whether Compaq's earlier success in managing "survivor syndrome" carries over to the new millennium.[6]

CISCO SYSTEMS, ACCENTURE, AND MOTOROLA

Strategy: Generate goodwill, even loyalty, among departing employees.

The United States has just sailed through five years of labor shortfalls on a scale not seen in more than three decades. What's more, the unemployment rate, while still rising, remains at historically low levels. Indeed, the unemployment rate for white-collar workers remains at just 2.2 percent.[7] Many employers are cautious about laying off too many workers, just to find themselves scrambling to refill the positions when demand picks up. To avoid that scenario, some are developing ingenious plans to "park" their most highly skilled employees until the economy recovers and to promote goodwill, even loyalty, among those they have to let go.

Cisco Systems, which is shrinking its staff to 30,500 from 38,000 and paying six months' salary to those who sign severance agreements, is also trying a 21st-century version of the old industrial furlough. In a pilot program, it is paying 70 employees one-third of their salaries while lending them to nonprofit organizations for a year. In effect, Cisco is warehousing them until they might be needed.[8] Despite the layoffs, Cisco still managed to rank 15th on *Fortune*'s 2002 list of the "Best 100 Companies to Work For": "During the layoffs, not one person I spoke to had a bad word to say about Cisco. That helps to explain how a company can lay off 5,500 and still make this list."[9]

Accenture, the former consulting arm of Andersen Worldwide, did cut 600 support staff in June 2001, but to retain skilled employees, it developed the idea of partially paid sabbaticals. The firm pays 20 percent of each employee's salary for 6 to 12 months, plus benefits, and it lets the employee keep his or her work phone number, laptop, and e-mail. About 1,000 employees took up the offer. Said Accenture's managing partner for internal operations, "This is a way to cut costs that gives us the ability to hang onto people we spent so much time recruiting and training."[10]

Motorola has been hard-hit by the global slowdown in telecommunications. As a result it is eliminating 30,000 jobs of the 147,000 that existed in January 2001, but at the same time it does not want to waste the results of its laborious recruiting during the late 1990s. Every laid-off employee in the United States is getting a minimum of eight weeks' pay as severance, a benefit that until the late 1990s was not so broadly available to lower-ranking employees.

Motorola has also become more active in sponsoring job fairs and outplacement clinics where those leaving the company can receive help in writing résumés, honing interviewing skills, and making contacts.[11] Why is Motorola going to such lengths to generate goodwill among departing employees? It views these initiatives as subtle tools for future recruiting, once the economy revives and hiring resumes.

All three of these companies are forsaking short-term savings in favor of longer-term payoffs from their relationships with current, former, and prospective employees. Their goal is simple: to become firms that people look to as "employers of choice."

STATE OF CONNECTICUT, DEPARTMENT OF LABOR, AND REFLEXITE CORPORATION

Strategy: Provide unemployment benefits for employees whose hours are cut.

How does this sound? You work for an employer that reduces your hours in an effort to avoid layoffs, so you get to keep your job and company benefits, including health insurance. At the same time, you collect unemployment benefits from the state to compensate you for the hours you are foregoing. The Connecticut Shared Work Program does just that.

The program is designed to meet the needs of companies that are experiencing a downturn in business but expect it to rebound. As of late 2001, 43 companies were participating in the program, with more applications pending. Here is how the program works.

During a formal application process, the company must inform employees and unions of the plan. Once the state Department of Labor approves the application, the company can participate in the program for up to one year. Instead of laying off one full-time worker, a company could instead reduce the hours of five other employees by one day each. Normally those workers would not qualify for unemployment pay, but under the Shared Work Program they can earn as much as 50 percent of their gross pay for the missed day. The company completes all requests for reimbursement and submits them directly to the state Department of Labor.

Said Tina McQuiggan, spokesperson for the Connecticut State Department of Labor, "The advantage for the employer[s] is that they get to retain their skilled work force. It also improves company morale because people aren't losing a full day or two of pay, they're getting it from us. They also avoid the emotional and financial hardships of being laid off. Most importantly, they retain their benefits. It really is a good program."[12]

This program shows how the public sector can work together with the private sector in a way that benefits both. It helps employers to retain the loyalty, commitment, and competencies of a trained workforce, and at the same time it allows workers to keep their jobs. One company that used a predecessor program, Connecticut's Voluntary Leave of Absence (LOA) program, in the early 1990s is Reflexite Corporation, an employee-owned firm with a Technology Center in Avon, Connecticut.

Reflexite's business is the management of light. It produces materials used in the manufacture of items such as street signs and reflective clothing used by fire, police, and road-building personnel. Its Reflective Products Business is the largest component of Reflexite Corporation, representing about half of its gross sales.[13] In

1991, although it was not losing customers or market share, the company faced declining sales as a result of the economic recession at that time. It went to great lengths to avoid layoffs. First, everyone took a cut in pay. Top management took a 10 percent cut, middle managers a 7 percent cut, and lower-level managers a 5 percent cut. All other employees took a 5 percent cut in the form of one day off per month without pay. On those days, the plant was closed.

Second, Reflexite developed a voluntary LOA plan in cooperation with the State of Connecticut. Under the plan, employees could take voluntary unpaid leaves of between two weeks and five months, while maintaining full benefits and receiving unemployment compensation from the state. In addition, those employees maintained their seniority and owners' bonus rights. They also had a guaranteed return date to the company.

About 90 employees participated in the program, saving the company over $400,000 in payroll costs (almost $600,000 in 2001 dollars). The combination of the voluntary LOA and the salary cuts produced 17 percent budget savings. In addition the company cut other manufacturing and administrative expenses dramatically, and a facility expansion was postponed.

These drastic measures worked. Reflexite avoided laying off even a single employee, business rebounded after the recession, and the company has been profitable every year since 1991.[14] In 1992, sales hit $30 million, and by 2000, sales had increased to $66 million. As a result of its experience, Reflexite goes to considerable lengths to disclose operating and strategic business information to its employees. One example is the Business Downturn Grid, a four-stage plan to be used during periods of slow business.

The premise behind the plan is to provide full disclosure to employees at every stage and to identify the symptoms that will trigger a particular course of action. Layoffs occur only at the fourth and final stage and are used as a last resort to save the company. Exhibit 7 shows Reflexite's Business Decline Contingency Plan. It contains four columns. The first names each stage of business decline, the second lists the symptoms that accompany each stage, the third describes actions to be taken, and the fourth lists expected results.

In recognition of the emphasis Reflexite places on employee involvement, it received two awards in 2000: the Ace Award for Communication Excellence from the ESOP Association, and the Business Leadership Award from the University of Hartford for its

EXHIBIT 7 Reflexite's Business Decline Contingency Plan

DEFINITION	SYMPTOMS	ACTIONS TO BE TAKEN	EXPECTED RESULTS
Stage 1: *Preventive*	1. Increased competitive activity 2. Capacity utilization down 3. Shipments below plan 4. Customer calls for requotes. 5. Customers delay or cancel orders. 6. Supplier shortages or excessive price increases 7. Field reports express concern. 8. Profits below plan for one month 9. Rumors of competitive product/knock-offs 10. Change at major customer	1. Communication from CEO 2. Review some budgeted hires. 3. Defer some budgeted activities. 4. Discuss at all team meetings. 5. Monitor overall economic conditions. 6. Review nonessential activity (i.e., wellness, WIT). 7. Double efforts on products under attack. 8. Accelerate key account plan activities. 9. Increase data collection. 10. Double efforts at key customers. 11. Enact midmonth forecasts from all business units.	• Adjust revenue and expenses to meet plan. • Get back on plan (YTD) within one month. • Meet the plan for the year.

| **Stage 2: Triage** | 1. Sales and profits below plan for two months
2. Keeping business through lower prices
3. Loss of key customer
4. New or existing customer introduces product attacking key Reflexite product offering.
5. External economic conditions on continued down trend
6. Key specification under consideration for rewrite
7. Larger customers' businesses decline or develop credit trouble. | 1. Increase communication.
2. Revise and submit for approval selling, general, and administrative (SG&A) expenditures—volume adjusted.
3. Implement across-the-board ideas to cut costs; improve productivity and efficiency from employees.
4. Defer hires that can't be funded through SG&A (volume adjusted) or hard dollars.
5. Increase cold calls.
6. Accelerate new product introductions.
7. Cut all nonessential activities and spending.
8. Increase sales force through nontraditional sales force.
9. Introduce a more aggressive revenue generation strategy. | • Preserve all jobs.
• Preserve stock value.
• Recapture lost customers.
• Meet plan for year.
• All employees rallying around recovery plan |

continued

EXHIBIT 7   *Continued*

DEFINITION	SYMPTOMS	ACTIONS TO BE TAKEN	EXPECTED RESULTS
Stage 3: *Operative*	1. Profits below prior year 2. Prediction of stock price decline 3. Continued trend decline for one quarter or break-even or loss for one month 4. Loss of several key customers 5. Bank loans increase. 6. Incentive pay plans dramatically reduced or not paid 7. Loss of employees 8. Competition attacking and taking market share	1. Voluntary leaves and furloughs 2. Hiring freeze 3. Revise plan and expenditures. 4. All budget variances reviewed on a regular basis 5. Defer lower-priority capital items. 6. Price cuts on specified items 7. Reduce inventories. 8. Offer extended terms for new business. 9. Continued emphasis on launching new products 10. Accelerate capital with less than one-year payout. 11. Defer raises. 12. Review and reduce labor hours. 13. Increase salary, work week hours.	• Reassure employees and shareholders. • Meet revised plan. • Preserve jobs. • Minimize stock decline. • Prevent future customer loss. • Regain customer confidence. • Get back on profit stream to support future investments. • All employees focused on recovery plan

Stage 4: Code Red	1. Continued loss of customers 2. Loss of technological lead 3. Continued loss of employees 4. Loss of shareholder confidence 5. Key products selling at consolidated GM below 25 percent 6. Banks look at loan status more carefully. 7. Business generates losses for two quarters or more. 8. Core products losing significant market share	1. Layoffs 2. Trim benefits. 3. Early retirements 4. Voluntary resignations offering 5. Stop all investments in future opportunities, and redeploy assets into short-term profit enhancement activities. 6. Review and reevaluate corporate strategy and direction. 14. Redeploy engineering capabilities into product development. 15. Approach suppliers to share in downturn.	• Downsizing required • Some loss of jobs • Minimize fall of stock price. • Continue to exist. • Get back on recovery plan and profits.

business results, commitment to employee development, and involvement in the local community.[15]

INTEL, CHEVRONTEXACO, AND MINNESOTA MINING AND MANUFACTURING COMPANY (3M)

Strategy: Ensure employment security through redeployment.

The idea of providing employment security—helping employees acquire marketable skills as jobs change—seems somehow old-fashioned or impossible in today's competitive world and very much at odds with what most firms seem to be doing. But employment security is fundamental to the implementation of most other high-performance work practices.[16] When employees are assured of continued employment, their commitment to their employers increases, and they share knowledge to enhance productivity. Knowing that they will use layoffs only as a last resort, employers, in turn, tend to hire sparingly.[17]

This is one major reason why some large companies, such as Intel, ChevronTexaco, and Minnesota Mining and Manufacturing Company (3M) engage in redeployment—providing other opportunities within the company for employees affected by restructuring. They do so by growing their businesses into new areas or by building on existing product lines or services.

Intel, the company that invented the computer microchip and whose average product life cycle is just 2.5 years, has avoided major layoffs through a strong in-house redeployment policy. When new technology makes some jobs obsolete, Intel provides choices to all of its employees who are performing satisfactorily. They can take advantage of self-assessment tools, career counseling, and job listings within Intel. The company also offers displaced employees opportunities for in-house training, job tryouts, even relocation to other Intel facilities. The entire process is managed through a system that provides centralized tracking and reporting of all redeployment activity.

The ranks of Intel employees are filled with those who have made successful transitions from shop floor to sales and public relations positions or from obsolete technology divisions to high-margin technology centers within the company. Intel benefits in two ways: it preserves institutional memory among employees who might otherwise be let go, and at the same time it develops more versatile employees who can contribute in multiple areas, especially as members of cross-functional teams.

If none of the job placement strategies is successful, then the company pays for outplacement assistance for affected employees.[18] Unfortunately, in 2001 Intel's employees were affected by more than just obsolete technology. The company was caught in the economic downdraft that swept the high-technology industry. As a result, even though senior managers received no pay increases, Intel still was forced to cut 7,000 jobs.[19] Sometimes layoffs are simply unavoidable.

ChevronTexaco also redeployed workers. As part of a major restructuring, it offered all affected employees an opportunity to participate in an effort that featured retraining and a chance for placement at ChevronTexaco subsidiaries. The company's cost reduction measures affected a broad spectrum of employees: geologists, engineers, technicians, pilots, secretaries, IT specialists, and offshore oil platform workers.[20]

One aspect of redeployment training focused on developing computer-based competencies. The company hired Manpower, Inc., a provider of temporary help and employment services, to conduct on-site classes in various word-processing, spreadsheet, and database management software. Over a six-week period, it conducted more than 200 computer-training sessions at Chevron's career center. Approximately 85 percent of the trainees found jobs subsequently.

Other company-sponsored programs include outplacement services (interviewing, résumé writing, networking), a 75 percent reimbursement for the cost of college tuition and books, and help for scientific professionals who wish to earn their teaching certificates at an accelerated pace. Although it was not possible to redeploy all affected workers, it did redeploy about 900 of them, thereby saving more than $25 million in severance costs alone.[21] In addition to providing employment security for departing employees, ChevronTexaco's actions provide important signals to those who continue to work at the company that they too can expect to be treated well if it ever becomes their turn to leave.

3M provides a final example of redeployment. When business lags at one of the company's 49 divisions, excess workers are employed at similar work in another division. Over the past decade,

3M has reassigned about 3,500 workers this way, failing to place only a handful, according to Richard Lindstad, vice president of human resources. "Our employees are corporate assets, not assets of a given business. It's like production machinery. In a downturn you don't just throw it out."[22]

ACXIOM, INC.

Strategy: Ask for *voluntary* pay cuts, plus other sacrifices from executives and employees alike. In return, issue shares of company stock.

As the recession that began in March of 2001 deepened, many firms imposed *mandatory* pay cuts on their employees. In the auto industry, both Ford Motor Company and Delphi Automotive Systems Corporation, the largest parts maker, suspended their matching contributions to employees' 401(k) savings plans. At the same time, Detroit-area businesses that supply car makers with engineering or administrative contract labor sliced such employees' wages, froze their merit raises, and weakened their health insurance benefits. Similar actions are taking place in the newspaper and airline industries, as this trend gains momentum.[23]

There is a substantial difference psychologically, however, between mandatory and voluntary pay cuts. Voluntary pay cuts provide employees with choice and some degree of control over events that affect them. As we have seen, such control reduces the effects of psychological and physical distress.[24]

Database management firm Acxiom of Little Rock, Arkansas, asked employees and managers to take voluntary pay reductions to help the company weather some economic hard times in 2001. It anticipated that 10 to 20 percent of the workforce might participate. After all, management already had imposed a mandatory 5 percent cut, and many employees might believe that they had already done their fair share. Needless to say, the company was "blown away" when it found that 36 percent, or 1,973 people had agreed to the reduction, losing about 5 percent of their paychecks.[25]

In this case, however, employees and managers were rewarded for their efforts. The money lost to mandatory and voluntary pay cuts has been returned to employees in the form of shares in the company's stock. The company offered a 1:1 ratio for the mandatory cuts and a 2:1 ratio for the voluntary ones. For example, if employee Harry Fox takes a voluntary $15,000 pay cut, he receives $30,000 in Acxiom stock. If he loses $8,000 as a result of the mandatory 5 percent cut, he receives company stock amounting to $8,000.

Was the program successful? Yes, for the company saved more than $24 million in 2001, it had no layoffs, and it gained a workforce vested in the success of Acxiom. Other forms of "share-the-pain" measures include taking unpaid vacations and working fewer hours per week.

These efforts sound humane, but they also make sound business sense. Most economists, such as Princeton University's Alan Blinder, former vice chairman of the Federal Reserve Board, generally agree that recessions last from 9 to 11 months. Companies that cut jobs at the first sign of trouble in their businesses simply will not be prepared to exploit growth opportunities when demand picks up.

That's a lesson that Acxiom president Charles Morgan learned the hard way. In 1991, he laid off 7 percent of his workforce. When the economy started its long and sustained climb upward in the 1990s, the company had to work twice as hard to find people to fuel its growth. Morgan is determined not to make the same mistake again.[26]

Voluntary (or mandatory) reductions in pay and some benefits do not guarantee success, however. Agilent Technologies, Inc., the $8.3 billion Palo Alto, California–based maker of test and measurement equipment that was spun off by Hewlett-Packard Company, imposed a three-month, mandatory, across-the-board pay cut of 10 percent in an effort to avoid layoffs altogether. It did so after the imposition of a hiring freeze, letting go about 5,000 temporary workers, and drastic cuts in travel expenses and equipment purchases. Those steps were not enough, as business worsened and losses mounted. In two rounds of layoffs, the company had to cut 8,000 people (27 percent of its staff at its peak), eliminate bonuses, and impose temporary 10 percent pay cuts on 1,800 senior managers. The process was managed extremely well. Employees being let go had to be told by their direct managers, and across-the-board job cuts were forbidden. Everything was handled division by division, looking at each program and each employee. Employees were kept informed through multiple rounds of regular communications from the CEO as well as from their immediate managers. Honesty and integrity were hallmarks of the process. Despite the company's problems, employees have supported the pay cuts and the share-the-pain philosophy.[27] Morale remains high. Said one Agilent employee, "It sounds hokey, but it's like a family. Everyone knows we have to chip in to make sure that everyone else is okay."[28]

SAGE SOFTWARE, INC.

Strategy: Rely on attrition, workforce planning, and rigorous performance reviews to adjust the size of the workforce regularly.

Sage has strong feelings about layoffs. Says vice president Beccie Dawson, "Layoffs show there's no company loyalty to employees, no stability, and they encourage the best and the brightest to start looking for new jobs."[29] She believes that layoffs signal a lack of management skill and little understanding of how head counts affect the bottom line. Here's how Sage uses that information.

In the software business, revenue per employee should be roughly $185,000 to $230,000 per year. Sage uses those numbers to determine precisely how many employees it should have based on quarterly sales. For example, say sales in the previous quarter were $8 million. If the average employee generates $210,000 in sales per year, that is $52,500 in sales per employee per quarter. Based on the quarterly revenues, the company needs about 150 employees.

At Sage, about 17 percent of the workforce leaves voluntarily every year. If sales decline, the company simply does not fill the vacated positions. In addition, the company's managers conduct rigorous performance reviews and eliminate poor performers on a routine basis. Hence, they adjust the size of the workforce regularly and do not have a lot of excess employees to worry about, should a downturn occur.

Darrell Rigby, a director at Bain & Company, the global consulting firm based in Boston, endorses the approach used at Sage. "On average, U.S. companies see voluntary employee turnover of 15 percent to 20 percent per year. Another 5 percent to 10 percent are probably bad placements. To me this says that companies experiencing volume declines of less than 10 percent can probably use a combination of cost reduction, intelligent hiring, voluntary turnover, and performance management to minimize the number of layoffs required."[30]

LOUISIANA-PACIFIC CORPORATION

Strategy: Costs need to be cut; let employees determine how to do it.

Payroll costs are certainly visible targets for cost cutting. Yet some companies have chosen to give their employees the opportunity to reach cost-cutting targets on their own. Louisiana-Pacific Corporation is one of them.

The 130 workers at the company's Chilco, Idaho, plant were shaken when Louisiana-Pacific announced in September 1998 that it would sell the plant. Company officials thought that further investment in the plant would be a waste of time and money. With many of the company's sawmills needing upgrading, Chilco was deemed too old to make the cut. The decades-old plant had been rebuilt in the early 1980s after a devastating fire but given little modern sawing equipment. It was one of many older mills that were simply neglected under a prior management regime. Said the company's lumber operations manager in the northern region, "Chilco was a loser, a bad loser."[31] At the time, the timber-based economy in Idaho was mired in a slump, with other mills in the region also feeling the economic pain. The slump was brought on, in part, by the federal government's closure of extensive national forest areas to further logging.

Rather than wait for the ax to fall, the employees of the Chilco plant decided to devise a comeback strategy. They figured that if they could achieve measurable production savings on their own, then the headquarters brass in Portland, Oregon, might give Chilco a reprieve and invest more money in the plant.

Unknown to management, the workers started making sure to use every last bit of wood. For example, a one-inch piece of lumber that normally would be considered too small for anything other than scrap was used to help make pallets. Boards with deformities that previously would have been junked were sawed carefully so parts could be used for lumber. Workers even made better use of the wood leavings. They figured out that if they used less water to lubricate the cutting saws, that would produce a drier, more valuable sawdust for making pulp and paper.

By Christmas of 1998, top officials at Louisiana-Pacific began to notice the changes at Chilco. "Good things were happening, and it was almost as if they were happening on their own," said a top manager who became familiar with the Chilco turnaround. As the company's management began putting together a capital-spending plan in early 1999, executives familiar with the turnaround at Chilco lobbied to have it included. A potent selling point was that the workers themselves had initiated and were committed to change.

As a result, Chilco was taken off the block. In July 1999, Louisiana-Pacific committed about $15 million to the Chilco plant for a five-year modernization effort. Since then, the company has modernized the aging plant, installing computerized saws and trimming equipment. By 2001, the changeover was about two-thirds complete, and the results were impressive. The Chilco sawmill jumped from one of Louisiana-Pacific's least efficient lumber mills to the best in its category. Productivity is so high that the plant produces 13 percent more lumber than before modernization, with roughly the same number of employees. According to Walt Wirfs, Louisiana-Pacific's vice president of lumber, "Usually you put money into a plant and get the work crew to take advantage of the new equipment. But at Chilco we had a crew demonstrating willingness to improve before we did anything. As a result, the learning curve was short."[32]

Management at Louisiana Pacific did not initiate this example of responsible restructuring. Rather, the workers themselves took the initiative to demonstrate to management that they were valuable assets whose creativity and ingenuity could improve productivity and efficiency at their plant. In the process, they saved their own jobs and ensured a more secure future for the plant.

PHILIPS ELECTRONICS SINGAPORE

Strategy: When low-end production must be relocated, work with the union to offer training, counseling, and job-finding assistance to retrenched workers.

Philips has operations in more than 60 countries in the areas of lighting, consumer electronics, domestic appliances, components, semiconductors, medical systems, business electronics, and information technology services. It began manufacturing operations in Singapore in 1969.[33]

Since the 1980s, manufacturing companies operating in Singapore have been following the global trend of relocating low-end production to lower-cost countries in the region. More recently, the trend has been to relocate to China and newly emerging economies with large supplies of low-cost labor and growing markets. In 1999, Philips Singapore took advantage of this opportunity to relocate part of its consumer electronics and domestic appliances business to China, Eastern Europe, and Mexico, thus lowering its operating costs while remaining based in Singapore. This restructuring exercise resulted in about 750 excess production operators, technicians, and related support staff.

In an effort to maintain a lean and flexible workforce in its low-end production in anticipation of an eventual relocation out of Singapore, Philips adopted the following human resource management strategies:

- Managers were required to assess long-term workforce projections carefully before recruiting new employees.
- Vacancies had to be filled from within the organization unless present staff could not meet the requirements.
- Philips recruited contract workers rather than full-time workers to meet increased demand and to provide flexibility when demand fluctuates.

When it became clear that the relocation would result in 750 excess employees, management informed the union, a branch of the Union of Workers in Electronics and Electrical Industries (UWEEI), of the situation. They worked together to ensure that the retrenched workers were given as much support and help as possible in finding alternative work.

Philips puts priority on employee self-development, with the belief that people are its most valuable resources. It has earned a reputation for being an enlightened and caring employer, having won several prestigious awards from the National Trade Union Congress (NTUC) and from the government. Its demonstrated commitment to its employees, as stated in its philosophy of management, is that employees should be

- respected,
- challenged,
- encouraged, and
- given equal opportunities.

Key Initiatives

Skills Upgrading and Training for Employability   Together with the UWEEI and the NTUC, Philips encouraged all of the affected workers to take advantage of a program that had been initiated by the NTUC, the Skills Redevelopment Program. That program provides attractive training grants to companies. Its objective is to help workers, especially those who were older and lower skilled, to become more employable through skills upgrading. Philips encouraged the 750 affected workers to enroll in the Certificate of Competence in Electronic Maintenance under the Skills Redevelopment Program.

Counseling and Employment Assistance   On the day the retrenchments were announced in December 1999, the company made sure that all affected workers were registered with the NTUC Employment Assistance Program and that company and union representatives were available to answer questions. Later, a job fair was organized by the Ministry of Manpower and union representatives to assist affected workers in their job search.

Job Matching   The first priority was to help workers secure alternative employment, by trying to match them with vacancies in job data banks kept by the NTUC Employment Assistance Program and the government-sponsored Employment Services Department. In an initial effort in December 1999, more than 30 retrenched workers were identified as having the necessary qualifications to pursue further training for a higher skills job such as wafer fabrication. The union approached ST Microelectronics, which had vacancies in this area, and got its agreement to interview interested workers. The union encouraged other workers who were qualified or interested to undergo training in order to qualify for higher-paying employment opportunities.

Financial Assistance   To minimize financial hardship, retrenchment benefits were paid according to the collective bargaining agreement: one month's pay for every year of service for those with three or more years of service, and one week's pay for every year for those with fewer than three years' service. In addition, workers received one month's pay in lieu of notice of retrenchment, and those retrenched in December still received the One-Month Annual Wage Supplement normally paid at the end of the year.

Outcomes

Many of the laid-off workers had worked for Philips for more than 20 years, and this had been their first job. They understood the company's need to reduce operating costs and to remain competitive. At the same time they appreciated the support provided both by the management and by the union in helping them to adjust to the sad reality. Such support also boosted the morale and confidence of those who continued to work in the plants.

PROCTER & GAMBLE COMPANY

Strategy: If layoffs become necessary, act in ways that are consistent with your corporate culture.

In 2001, Procter & Gamble Company (P&G), the maker of Tide, Pampers, and Crest, among other products, began the process of eliminating 5,600 jobs in the United States, the largest white-collar cut in its 163 years. In an effort to minimize the number of involuntary job cuts, the company offered a buyout package to approximately 20,000 nonmanufacturing employees, or about half its domestic workforce. In effect, it asked for volunteers from this segment of its workforce, hoping to boost morale among the remaining employees.

Under the buyout package, U.S. employees who have worked for P&G for at least a year are eligible for benefits that include severance pay, health care, outplacement assistance, and retraining reimbursement, depending on how long they have been at P&G. Employees were given about two months to request information about the package. Once they did, they had 45 days from the time they received the information to decide whether to leave, plus a week afterward to change their minds. They could also decide how long to continue working after they decided to depart.

The advantage to taking the voluntary buyout is personal control. Those who are laid off will receive the same benefits, but they cannot set the timing of their departure. As we have seen, personal control reduces stress and increases one's sense of self-determination.

After the CEO announced the voluntary buyout program, he asked all employees to meet with their bosses in the following 10 days to discuss their place in a leaner P&G. For much of the ensuing two months, P&G hosted two information sessions daily to sell its "employee-initiated separation package." Each two-hour session typically drew about 100 attendees. P&G emphasized that there would be no stigma attached to employees who reviewed a package but decided to stay.

At the same time, some P&G bosses worried that their star employees might leave. The president of P&G's global pharmaceutical business did more than worry. He made time every day to meet individually with managers to praise them and sell them on a future at P&G.

The company believes that its program works for its business and its culture. It typically hires managers straight out of school and promotes from within. Most executives have never worked anywhere else, and most haven't written a résumé or job hunted since their early 20s.

P&G's strategy is humane, but it is not without costs. For one thing, the voluntary process takes months. Employees and managers alike are distracted as they attend various information seminars about the buyout on company time. Planning future assignments can be tricky because managers aren't sure who will be around.[34]

On the other hand, Dick Antoine, P&G's global head of human resources, commented, "I am absolutely convinced that this is right for our shareholders and for our people." P&G gave workers a similar amount of time to adjust to leaving when cutting manufacturing jobs since the 1980s, and productivity never suffered. The generous time frame fits P&G's core value of respect for individuals. Still, he acknowledges, "Are we paying a little more? Perhaps. Are we dragging it out a little? Perhaps."[35] The bottom line: P&G believes that it is worth the additional cost and time to act in ways that are consistent with its corporate culture.

6

The Virtues of Stability

While it is currently fashionable to lay off employees as a way of becoming "more competitive," some companies have steered an alternate course. In their view, there is virtue in providing stability and employment security.

Do you recall the research described in chapter 2 on the financial consequences of employment downsizing from 1982–2000? In that study, Stable Employers, those whose complement of employees did not fluctuate by more than plus or minus 5 percent, were more profitable in the year of the announcement of the cuts and in the ensuing two years than Employment Downsizers. This finding held up even after adjusting for the performance of the industry in which each firm competes. A second finding was that downsizing firms did not perform any better than Stable Employers with respect to the total return on their common stock. This was also true on an industry-adjusted basis.

Could it be that there is virtue in stability? Eighty of the 100 companies that made *Fortune*'s 2002 list of the "100 Best Companies to Work For" avoided layoffs in 2001; 47 of them even have some kind of official policy *barring* layoffs! Consider stockbroker Edward Jones, the number one firm on the list. Although it was hit particularly hard by the gloomy stock market, it responded by cutting back bonuses. None of its 25,000 employees got the ax. Says Jones's CEO, John Bachmann, "We want to build the kind of relationship with workers that makes them willing to go the extra mile. You can't do that if you get rid of them whenever times are rocky." The lesson is simple: no matter how rough the economy, retaining top talent is a huge issue. In fact, losing key people during downturns can be disastrous.[1]

The fact is that a tiny minority of firms in the United States have a practice of not laying off employees—period. As a result, such firms never have to deal with the fact that layoffs leave a company traumatized and unfocused. They don't ever have to worry about whether the surviving employees are distracted and less productive because of worries about the security of their own employment. In companies with employment security, employees are not afraid to be innovative and to take risks, because they know that honest efforts will not be punished. Skills and contacts that have been nurtured over the years can be maintained. As an example, consider Intuit, the maker of Quicken personal financial software. When a new product failed, the company threw a "Failure Celebration" to help the team learn from its mistakes![2]

Think about it. Companies can maintain their special efficiencies only if they can give their workers a unique set of skills and a feeling that they belong together. Teams work best if the team members get to know and trust each other and if each team member masters a broad enough range of skills to be able to double-up for absent colleagues. Profit-sharing makes sense only if the employees are around at the end of the year to enjoy their rewards.[3]

In fact, there was a time when working for a large company guaranteed employment security. The benefit to the company was employee loyalty. In the 1980s, for example, IBM had to renege on its no-layoff policy after being blindsided by the revolution in desktop computers, causing deep resentment among employees. The trend today is to view employees as bundles of skills who are responsible for their own careers. Many corporations view them as any other commodity or service. However, a small number of other firms see hidden costs in distancing people. They recognize that the most successful firms of this or the past century have been those that recognize the value of their people. They believe that employees who feel appreciated will be motivated, innovative, and productive.[4] They will go the extra mile to make their companies successful through discretionary actions that may not even be recognized formally by their companies. Such actions are known as organizational citizenship behaviors, or simply OCBs.[5] OCBs can take many forms, but the major ones include the following:

- Altruism (e.g., helping out when a coworker is not feeling well)
- Conscientiousness (e.g., staying late to finish a project)
- Civic virtue (e.g., volunteering for a community program to represent the firm)
- Sportsmanship (e.g., sharing the failure of a team project that would have been successful if the team had followed your advice)
- Courtesy (e.g., being understanding and empathetic, even when provoked)[6]

For employees to demonstrate OCBs, they must perceive that they are being treated fairly, that procedures and outcomes are fair. Such perceptions affect employees by influencing their sense of organizational support, which then prompts them to reciprocate with OCBs, going beyond their formal job requirements.[7]

Obviously, OCBs are valuable to organizations, even though they frequently go undetected by the reward system. OCBs relate clearly both to job satisfaction and to organizational commitment. Individuals who exhibit OCBs perform better and receive higher performance evaluations. OCBs also relate to group and organization performance and effectiveness.[8] Stable organizations that provide employment security enhance the job satisfaction and commitment of their employees, and make it more likely that OCBs will emerge.

SNAP BACK

It's not just corporate altruism at work in stable employers. Rather, executives at no-layoff companies argue that maintaining their ranks even in terrible times breeds fierce loyalty, higher productivity, and the innovation needed to enable them to snap back once the economy recovers. For example, following the September 11, 2001, tragedy, the Boeing Company announced that it would slash 30,000 jobs, slash jet deliveries from about 600 to 300 in the next two years, and lift outsourcing to more than 60 percent of components, up from 49 percent. The planned cuts immediately antagonized Boeing's two biggest unions, which accused the company of sacrificing people for profit. Two months after the company's announcement, union proposals to dampen the impact with early-retirement packages, voluntary layoffs, or less outsourcing to contractors went nowhere.

At the same time, Boeing expects orders to rebound by 2003, lifting production rates back above 500 planes a year. Will it be able to snap back when the industry recovers? A recent study by Massachusetts Institute of Technology found that the aerospace industry already has cut 500,000 jobs since 1990 and has not done enough to replace an aging workforce. This suggests that the steep layoffs could leave Boeing woefully short of skilled workers if orders do rebound as the company expects.[9]

Some private companies such as S. C. Johnson, Third Federal Savings & Loan, and Pella have long traditions that date back to the Great Depression when workers washed windows over and over just to stay busy. Privately held Publix Supermarkets (128,742 employees) hasn't had a single layoff in 71 years. Bank and credit card processor Synovus Financial of Columbus, Georgia, hasn't had a layoff in 114 years! Other public companies—such as Federal Express (176,389 employees), AFLAC, Erie Insurance, Xilinx (a Silicon Valley maker of programmable logic chips), stockbroker Edward Jones, Vanguard Group, and Nucor—rely on creative cost cutting. Size alone, or public versus private status, is no barrier to such policies.

At steelmaker Nucor, based in Charlotte, North Carolina, some plants are on a four-day schedule, shaving 20 percent off the average worker's $50,000 annual pay. Bonuses of senior executives, which make up 66 percent of their salaries, have been wiped out, too.

Some newcomers to the policy say they were won over after battling the brutal war for talent in the late 1990s. For example, San Francisco law firm Brobeck, Phleger & Harrison, whose fortunes swelled with the dot.com boom, struggled through the worst business climate in its 76-year history in 2001. Still, the firm stuck to its no-layoff rule by eliminating Town Cars, expense accounts, travel and partner retreats. Executives at no-layoff companies want to make layoffs the last place they look—instead of the first.[10]

According to Frederick Reichheld, author of two books on loyalty, stable companies that provide employment security have a deep appreciation of how employee loyalty drives down costs.[11] They also have the advantage of having long taken a conservative approach to both cash and debt. In this chapter, we highlight three such firms: Lincoln Electric Holdings, Inc., the SAS Institute, and Southwest Airlines. It is important to emphasize that while such companies may restructure from time to time, restructuring does not include layoffs as part of the equation.

LINCOLN ELECTRIC HOLDINGS, INC.

From its earliest years, 100-year-old Lincoln Electric Holdings, Inc., of Cleveland, Ohio, has charted a unique path in worker–management relations, featuring high wages, guaranteed employment, few supervisors, a lucrative bonus-incentive system, and piecework compensation. The company is the world's largest maker of arc-welding equipment; it has 3,400 U.S. employees, 23 plants in 17 countries, and no unions. The Harvard Business School has cited Lincoln Electric as a sterling model of corporate responsibility, and many observers of the labor scene have justifiably praised its innovative management practices. Here are some that set Lincoln apart:[12]

- Guaranteed employment for all full-time workers with three or more years of service, regardless of economic conditions. No worker has been laid off since 1948, and turnover is less than 5 percent for those with more than three years on the job.

- High wages plus a substantial annual bonus (up to 100 percent of base pay) based on the company's profits. Wages at Lincoln are roughly equivalent to wages for similar work elsewhere in the Cleveland area, but the bonuses the company pays make its compensation substantially higher. The most hard-driving workers make over $100,000. Lincoln has never had a strike and has not missed a bonus payment since the system was instituted in 1934. Individual bonuses are set by a formula that judges workers on five dimensions: quality, output, dependability, ideas, and cooperation. The ratings determine how much of the total corporate bonus pool each worker will get, on top of his or her hourly wage.

- Piecework is common—more than half of Lincoln's workers are paid according to what they produce, rather than an hourly or weekly wage. If a worker is sick, he or she does not get paid.

- Promotion is almost exclusively from within, according to merit, not seniority.

- Few supervisors, with a supervisor-to-worker ratio of 1 to 100, far lower than in much of the industry. Each employee is supposed to be a self-managing entrepreneur, and each is accountable for the quality of his or her own work.

- No formal break periods, mandatory overtime, and flexibility in assignments are allowed. These policies apply only to Lincoln's U.S. employees. Employees must work overtime, if ordered to, during peak production periods and must agree to be reassigned to any division within the company to meet production schedules or to maintain the company's guaranteed employment program. The company provides a considerable amount of cross training and transfers someone to a new position almost every day. A reassigned employee receives the wage of the new job, which, in some cases, can be as much as $5 an hour less than their previous pay.

- While the company insists on individual initiative—and pays according to individual effort—it works diligently to foster the notion of teamwork. And it did so long before the Japanese became known for emphasizing such concepts. If a worker is overly competitive with fellow employees, he or she is rated poorly in terms of cooperation and team play on his or her semiannual rating reports. Thus, that worker's bonus will be smaller. Indeed, Lincoln's performance appraisal system is so rigorous that as many as half of first-year workers either do not make the cut or else they decide on a different career.

What happens in an economic downturn? In the 1980s, when domestic sales plummeted 40 percent, the company took 50 volunteer workers off the shop floor, retrained them, and sent them into the field as salespeople. They called on distributors, and within the company they were known as "leopards," because they were finding spots in the market that the company had not covered. Many had college degrees and today still work in sales. For example, the leopards discovered a market for home-welding equipment, the kind that could be used on small welding jobs, such as repairing backyard barbecues. Today that new line of business is contributing a steady stream of new revenues that did not exist before the leopards discovered a need for it.

This is an excellent example of responsible restructuring because instead of asking, "What's the irreducible core number of employees we need to run our business?" Lincoln asked, "How can we change the way we do business so that we can use our current employees more effectively?"

Lincoln makes a good business case for avoiding layoffs, but vice president of HR Ray Vogt says there's a humane philosophy that aligns with the strategy of the business. "The more typical response is to push for layoffs, but you'll find that destroys the fabric of the workforce. Lincoln shows how a different process can work, but it requires more creativity and imagination. This approach takes more time and more thought. It's just as tough-minded as layoffs, yet humane because it takes away the anxiety of employees who will [otherwise] wonder, 'What happens to me when the economy goes down?'"[13]

SAS INSTITUTE

SAS Institute, the largest privately owned software company in the world, is a dinosaur. Here's how *Fast Company* magazine described SAS: "In an era of relentless pressure, this place is an oasis of calm. In an age of frantic competition, this place is methodical and clearheaded. In a world of free agency, signing bonuses, and stock options, this is a place where loyalty matters more than money."[14]

In almost every respect, SAS Institute seems like a throwback to an earlier era, to a time when there were long-term attachments between companies and their people. At that time large, progressive organizations such as Eastman Kodak, S. C. Johnson, and Sears offered generous, inclusive benefits in an effort to enhance the welfare of their workforces.[15]

Not everyone seems to approve of this type of employment relationship. Some people say that SAS Institute reeks of paternalism or a plantation mentality in a world otherwise dominated by marketlike labor market transactions.[16] Of course, no one is forced to work at the company, and since it is located in Cary, in the Research Triangle area of North Carolina, it is surrounded by numerous pharmaceutical companies, as well as by IBM, Northern Telecom, and many other high-technology and software companies. SAS people would not even have to move geographically if they wanted to change jobs!

Yet SAS Institute, with no signing bonuses, no stock options, no phantom stock—none of the gimmicks that have come to be taken for granted as ways of inducing people to join and remain at companies—has a turnover rate of less than 4 percent. In the software industry in particular, turnover is endemic and seems inevitable. Annual employee turnover of 20 percent is typical. Job hopping is an accepted, and even expected, part of people's career strategy. But not at SAS.

The Company

SAS Institute was founded in 1976 by Dr. James Goodnight, John Sall, Anthony Barr, and Jane Helwig. As a student at North Carolina State University, Goodnight worked on the university's statistical analysis package. The objective was to develop a uniform computer program that could be used over and over and that could solve lots of different kinds of statistical problems. The partners obtained the rights to the original SAS software from North Carolina State University in return for providing free upgrades to the University.

When the SAS Institute began in 1976 as an independent entity, it already had 100 paying customers and a positive cash flow. Thus, it was able to begin business without any venture capital. Today, Goodnight is the CEO and owns two-thirds of the company, and Sall owns the remaining third. He remains as a software developer. The other two founders sold out earlier and left the company.

Over the years the SAS program has expanded to become a 25-module system for data warehousing, data mining, and decision support. Fully 98 of the Fortune 100 companies use it, as do 80 percent of the Fortune 500. Its overall customer base exceeds 8,000. Banks use SAS Institute software to do credit scoring, hotels use it to manage frequent-visitor programs, and the U.S. Census Bureau uses it to count and categorize the population.

The company operates on a worldwide basis, with 40 sales offices in the United States, 68 offices around the world, and licensed distributors in a number of other countries. It has experienced double-digit revenue growth over the past 24 years, and today it is a $1.12 billion company that employs about 7,500 people. Even as many technology-based companies struggled in 2000, SAS Institute grew its revenues an astounding 10.1 percent. SAS Institute has no debt (except for a mortgage on its first building) and has never had to raise outside venture or other equity capital. It spends more than 30 percent of its revenues on research and development, an amount that is about twice the average for the software industry.

Such investments clearly have paid off, as SAS has received several recent awards for its business intelligence software. Its e-Intelligence product was named "2000 Product of the Year" by *Customer Inter@action Solutions* magazine. *Start* magazine named the SAS Institute as one of 2001's "Hottest Companies," praising the firm for its achievements in delivering technology solutions to the manufacturing industry. It also noted, "SAS has clearly demonstrated the ability to persevere during a period when many technology providers could not."[17]

Strategy

Unlike many software vendors, SAS does not *sell* its products and subsequent upgrades but rather offers site licenses, provided on an annual basis after a 30-day trial. A charge of $50,000 per year for 50 users is typical.[18] However, the licenses include free upgrades to new versions of the software and outstanding customer support (one technical support person for every 100 customers). Its business is built on forming close, lasting relationships with customers, and customer loyalty is intense. The company's license renewal rate exceeds 98 percent.

To acquire new ideas, the company sponsors user group conferences. There are six regional user groups in the United States, one international group, and a dozen country-specific groups. In essence, the company's product development strategy is to stay in very close contact with customers and to give them what they want and need. Each year the company sends each of its customers a "ballot" asking what features they would like to see. From tabulating the results of that ballot, SAS Institute decides on its development priorities for the coming year.

Managing People

SAS Institute has operated the same way since its inception, based on a desire to create a corporation where it is as much fun for the workers as for top management. To do that, SAS manages people according to three core values and beliefs.

1. **Treat all people at SAS Institute fairly and equally**. SAS is a very egalitarian place, with no reserved parking places, no executive dining rooms, private offices (not cubicles) for everyone, and casual dress. Everyone eats at one of the on-site, subsidized cafeterias, accompanied by a pianist who plays during lunch.

2. **Make work fun, and treat people with dignity and respect**. Goodnight and other leaders all share in the belief that if you take care of your people, they will take care of the company.

3. **Rely on people's intrinsic motivation, and trust them to do a good job**. Barrett Joyner, vice president of North American Sales and Marketing, has stated that "the emphasis is on coaching and mentoring rather than on monitoring and controlling. Trust and respect—it's amazing how far you can go with that."[19]

The importance placed on people stems from the fact that SAS Institute operates in a business critically dependent on intellectual capital. David Russo, who was head of human resources for more than 17 years, explained:

> Every night at 6 o'clock, all of our assets walk out the door. . . . We just hope they come back at nine the next morning. . . . If you believe that, then it's just a waterfall of common sense. It just means that you take care of the folks who are taking care of you. . . . *Why* we do the things we do is what's important. The things we do are secondary. . . . They are just a natural outgrowth of a philosophy that if you really mean that your people are important, you will treat them like they are important.[20]

On the 25th anniversary of the company's founding, Goodnight remarked, "We knew that if we focused on our employees and our customers, the company would prosper. It sounded simplistic then, just as it does today, but I think history has shown that taking care of employees has made the difference in how our employees take care of our customers. With that as our vision, the rest takes care of itself."[21]

Benefits and the Work Environment

SAS Institute is justifiably famous for its generous, family-friendly benefits, and pleasant physical work environment. Twelve times *Working Mother* magazine has selected SAS Institute for its list of the 100 best companies for working mothers. Not surprisingly, *Fortune* magazine consistently has ranked the SAS Institute as one of the top 10 of its "100 Best Companies to Work For" in America. Company headquarters at Cary consists of 18 buildings scattered over 200 acres of a campuslike setting with a lake and beautiful forests. The buildings are light, airy, and architecturally interesting.

Company policy is for people to work about 35 hours per week, or a 9-to-5 work day, with an hour for lunch and exercise. The reduced work hours permit people to have both a job and a life. About half of SAS's managers are women, and it has been able to attract and retain both men and women with its work-life balance.

The company also provides a 7,500-square-foot on-site medical facility and a full-indemnity health plan—not an HMO or a PPO based on the concept of managed care. It also provides on-site day care, with one staff person for every three children, plus a fitness center that is free to employees and their families, benefits to domestic partners, and on-site help in arranging elder care. It does not outsource noncore activities such as health care, day care, food service, or security. Even in the cost-cutting environment that characterizes so many of today's companies, SAS Institute has maintained the special employee benefits that it is known for.[22] For employees not working at Cary, the company makes every effort to provide a similar level of benefits and amenities, either on-site for employees or by purchasing them from local vendors.

Performance Management and Pay

The company's fundamental approach to performance management is to set high expectations for both conduct and performance and then to give people freedom to do what they like to meet these expectations. Everyone gets regular, informal feedback about their performance, and managers are evaluated on their ability to attract and retain talent. In a business based on skill and know-how, SAS believes that if it can find and keep the best people, the rest will take care of itself.

Base salaries are competitive with industry standards, although people have taken pay cuts to work at SAS Institute because they value the work environment so highly. Annual bonuses are modest (5 to 8 percent). There are no stock options or similar schemes, and salespeople do not work on commission. SAS Institute provides heavy emphasis on training, but almost all of it is done internally. SAS believes that people will have three or four careers during their working lives—and it would like for all of them to be within SAS!

SAS Institute has a strong company culture, and fit is important in hiring, promotion, and retention decisions. It looks for people who will be team players, not those who seek to stand out or who want to be treated like stars. At SAS Institute, *everyone* is important, and the contributions of all of its people are valued and recognized.

This approach to people management is supported by the results of a recent survey by Space Transportation Systems, one of the few organizations in the world to achieve SEI-CMM Level 5 (a software industry measure of process quality).[23] The company was surprised to find that employees rated human issues as most important, not pay. Employees valued achievement and recognition highest, followed by project assignment and responsibility, and then opportunity for growth and advancement. At Fannie Mae, an internal poll found that employees gave top priority to controlling their own schedules. That includes the capacity to set priorities for day-to-day work, to select approaches for doing work, and to make decisions about resources. Clearly, SAS's approach to managing people is fully consistent with these findings.

We noted earlier that employee turnover at SAS Institute is very low, about 4 percent per year, compared to the software industry average of 20 percent. Given the size of its workforce, plus about 1.5 times annual salary to replace a person who leaves, the 16 percent less turnover that SAS enjoys, relative to its competitors, means that it realizes opportunity savings in excess of $100 million *every year*. SAS Institute is a stable employer that recognizes that there is virtue in stability.

SOUTHWEST AIRLINES

The story of Southwest Airlines is "rags to riches" if ever there was one. It started as a doodle on a cocktail napkin at a San Antonio, Texas, bar in 1966. By 2001, it had become the most successful airline in history. San Antonio lawyer Herb Kelleher founded Southwest with one of his clients, Rollin King (now a board member). At the time, the idea was revolutionary: a cut-rate airline that would fly between Dallas, San Antonio, and Houston. No one—not even Kelleher—was sure it would work. Indeed, its competitors were determined to make sure that it did not. From the moment the company was created, they used every legal and political strategy available to keep Southwest grounded. For the first 10 years of the company's life, Kelleher, then a board member and the company's lawyer, spent most of his days in court defending Southwest against lawsuits from the likes of Texas International and Braniff Airlines.[24]

In the early days, Southwest had limited resources for marketing. It gained attention by putting its flight attendants in hot pants and using its location at Dallas's Love Field as the theme of an advertising campaign ("Make Love, Not War"). It still uses that theme today when Southwest refers to itself as the "Love" (LUV) airline. This designator is Southwest's stock ticker symbol. All aircraft have a small heart emblazoned on their sides, and hearts are used prominently on corporate communications and advertising. From its inception, Southwest encouraged its employees to identify with others at the company, deliver great customer service, and have fun. Its aggressive, underdog spirit still pervades the company, especially among the longer-serving employees.[25] Even today, the company recognizes the value of its culture, and it strives fiercely to maintain it. "It's a matter of getting buy-in from each new hire, making it a culture they want to be a part of. We start from day one, trying to make people understand that we are looking for people who want to join a cause, not get a paycheck.[26]

Kelleher became chairman in 1978 and CEO in early 1982. At that time, the airline had just 27 planes, $270 million in revenues, 2,100 employees, and flew to 14 cities. Today, Southwest is a $5.6 billion business with 33,000 employees, and it serves 58 cities from Baltimore, to Nashville, to Los Angeles. At $14 billion, Southwest's market capitalization is bigger than American's,

United's, and Continental's combined.[27] Here's what *Fortune* magazine had to say shortly before Kelleher stepped down as CEO and president in June 2001:

> But what is most stunning of all about Southwest is that since 1973, when it first turned a profit, the company hasn't lost a penny. In an industry plagued by fare wars, recessions, oil crises, and other disasters, this is an astounding feat. No other airline has even come close to it. Even during the Persian Gulf War, when every other carrier gushed red ink, Southwest made money. In just this past quarter, because of rising jet-fuel prices, five of the largest air carriers—including Delta, United, and American—lost money. Southwest made $121 million in net profits—up 65 percent from a year ago.[28]

At the end of the first quarter of 2002, a dire time for U.S. airlines, only Southwest among the nine major carriers achieved any profit at all.[29]

Business Strategy

From the beginning to the present, Southwest has maintained the same strategy and operating style. It concentrates on flying to airports that are underused and close to a metropolitan area. It also flies only one type of aircraft, fuel-efficient 737s, which simplifies maintenance and training. At the end of 2001, it had 355 737s, with an average age of the fleet of just 8.6 years.[30] Southwest service involves frequent on-time departures and low-cost fares. It emphasizes point-to-point routes, with no central hub and an average flight time of 80 minutes.

By avoiding the hub-and-spoke system, Southwest is able to avoid the systemwide delays that often plague connecting flights through hub airports that experience bad weather. This makes short-haul trips more attractive to customers who might otherwise consider driving. The company offers no preassigned seating and no meals. It bills itself as a "no frills" airline, yet it is typically the leading carrier in passenger boardings at the airports it serves. Southwest has almost 70 percent of the intra-Texas market, about three-quarters of the intra-Florida market, and more than 50 percent of the intra-California traffic.[31]

It all seems so simple. So why haven't competitors been able to mimic the Southwest model? Many have tried, including America West, Reno Air, Kiwi Air, United, Continental, USAirways Group, and Delta. At least on the surface, there is little that the competition does not know. They understand the technology, cost structures, and route planning. The have the same equipment, locations, and marketing savvy. Yet over and over, whether large or small, Southwest's competitors have been unable to replicate its success.

One secret is in the remarkable productivity of Southwest's employees, plus a company culture that emphasizes having fun at work and absolute respect for people, whether those people are employees or customers. Another secret is shrewd management. As Kelleher noted, "Most people think of us as this flamboyant airline, but we're really very conservative from the fiscal standpoint. We have the best balance sheet in the industry. We've always made sure that we never over-reached ourselves. We never got dangerously in debt and never let costs get out of hand."[32]

In terms of productivity, consider these startling statistics. In 1998, Southwest had an average of 94 employees per aircraft (the total number of planes divided by the total number of employees), whereas United and American had almost 160. The industry average exceeded 130. Southwest served an average of more than 2,500 passengers per employee, whereas United and American served fewer than 1,000, about the industry average. Southwest thus needs a much smaller load factor to break even. It turns around 70 percent of its aircraft in 15 minutes or less (from the time a plane arrives at the gate until it leaves), as compared with the industry average of 35 minutes. Another cost advantage comes from having people who will do as many different tasks as required to get the flights out. Flight attendants and pilots will help clean the aircraft, load bags, or check passengers in at the gate.[33] Can you think of another airline where that happens?

Southwest's employees, including pilots, are not the highest paid in the industry. At the same time, the airline is 84 percent unionized, yet Southwest has signed record-breaking 10- and 12-year labor agreements with its pilots' and dispatchers' unions, respectively. Colleen Barrett, Kelleher's former legal secretary and now president of Southwest Airlines, is adamant about treating employees as internal customers and tries to make Southwest a comfortable and fun place to work. The results are undeniable.

Southwest has won the U.S. Department of Transportation's coveted Triple Crown (best on-time performance, fewest lost bags, and fewest customer complaints) seven times.

Working at Southwest is a fun experience, and humor is a core value of the culture. Serious attention is paid to parties and celebrations. The Love Field corporate headquarters in Dallas is filled with banners and with pictures of Southwest employees at parties, awards, trips, and celebrations. As Southwest notes in a section of its mission statement:

> We are committed to provide our employees a stable work environment with equal opportunity for learning and personal growth. Creativity and innovation are encouraged for improving the effectiveness of Southwest Airlines. Above all, employees will be provided the same concern, respect, and caring attitude within the organization that they are expected to share externally with every Southwest Customer.[34]

Lots of companies say their people are important. Southwest demonstrates this commitment through its actions. Here's what CEO Kelleher said as he was preparing to step down in June 2001:

> You have to treat your employees like your customers. When you treat them right, they will treat your outside customers right. That has been a powerful competitive weapon for us. . . . My mother taught me that. She was an extraordinary person. When I was very young—11 or 12—she used to sit up talking to me till three, four in the morning. She talked a lot about how you should treat people with respect. She said that positions and titles signify absolutely nothing. They're just adornments; they don't represent the substance of anybody. I was kind of her disciple. I learned firsthand what she was telling me was correct, because there was a very dignified gentleman in our neighborhood, the president of a local savings and loan, who used to stroll along in a very regal way up until he was indicted and convicted of embezzlement. She taught me that every person and every job is worth as much as any other person and any other job.[35]

Treating people with dignity and respect means driving out fear for one's employment security. Not only has Southwest never had a layoff or furlough—quite unusual in the airline industry—but it doesn't punish honest mistakes. Its official policy states, "No employee will ever be punished for using good judgment and good old common sense when trying to accommodate a customer—no matter what our other rules are."[36]

With respect to employment security, Kelleher commented in June 2001:

> The thing that would disturb me most to see after I'm no longer CEO is layoffs at Southwest. Nothing kills your company's culture like layoffs. Nobody has ever been furloughed here, and that is unprecedented in the airline industry. It's been a huge strength of ours. It's certainly helped us negotiate our union contracts. . . . We could have furloughed at various times and been more profitable, but I always thought that was shortsighted. You want to show your people that you value them and you're not going to hurt them just to get a little more money in the short term. Not furloughing people breeds loyalty. It breeds a sense of security. It breeds a sense of trust. So in bad times you take care of them, and in good times they're thinking, perhaps, "We've never lost our jobs. That's a pretty good reason to stick around."[37]

Kelleher would be pleased to know that in the wake of the September 11, 2001, attacks, as competitors announced job cuts of 20 percent, Southwest executives were packed into an emergency command center at their bare-bones Dallas headquarters, scheming to cut costs. Growth strategies were scotched. Deliveries of new planes were delayed. The renovations at headquarters were scrapped. But with $1 billion in cash and no debt, layoffs never had to be considered. Said new CEO James F. Parker, "We are willing to suffer some damage, even to our stock price, to protect the jobs of our people."[38]

Southwest has been recognized as a top-10 employer among *Fortune*'s list of "America's Most Admired Companies" since the program began in 1993. *Fortune* also has listed Southwest as one of the most admired companies in the world, year after year. It should come as no surprise that lots of people want to work at Southwest. In 2000, Southwest reviewed 216,000 résumés and hired 5,134 new employees. It is truly an employer of choice.

BEST EMPLOYERS IN ASIA

The people management practices that we have been describing thus far are similar to those of the best employers in Asia. In a joint effort, Hewitt Associates, together with *The Asian Wall Street Journal* and the *Far Eastern Economic Review*, surveyed 92,000 employees from 355 organizations in 10 different countries/regions for the Best Employers in Asia study that was completed in late 2001.[39] Results indicated that the top 10 firms were Portman Ritz-Carlton (China), Agilent Technologies (Singapore), Ritz-Carlton Millenia (Singapore), Western Digital (Malaysia), P. T. Elegant Textile (Indonesia), Federal Express (Malaysia), Tricon Restaurants (Thailand), Ritz-Carlton (Hong Kong), AMD (Thailand), and Navion Software (China).

What Distinguishes the Best of the Best?

The top employers share three characteristics:

- Clear vision (they know what they want to achieve and how to communicate it)
- Excellent delivery and execution of people-related initiatives
- Highly engaged employees who are aligned to the business strategies of their companies

For example, communications from the CEO occur 3.2 times more frequently in the Best Companies than in Other Companies, and 91 percent of Best Companies (vs. 76 percent of Other Companies) say their leaders have a good understanding of the direction and goals of the business. The Best Employers are great believers in values and culture, they provide work-life balance, fair pay, lots of recognition of their employees, they are open and honest in their communications, and their leaders are open and accessible.

In return, Best Employers enjoy the advantages of a loyal workforce that takes great pride in belonging to an organization that has built an excellent reputation. Employees of the Best Employers do more than just go to work and collect their pay. They feel they belong. They feel empowered. They recommend their own company's products and services, and they regard their employers so highly that they would recommend their friends to join the organization. They communicate these views throughout their respective communities. Here are the top five answers that distinguish the best of the best: [40]

	BEST EMPLOYERS (%)	OTHER COMPANIES (%)
"I feel that this organization is an exceptional place to work"	83	56
"I am able to influence what happens in this organization"	64	37
"Compared with other places where I might work, I feel I'm fairly paid"	72	45
"I am fairly paid for the contribution I make to our organization's success"	72	45
"I hardly ever think about leaving this organization to work somewhere else"	72	45

THE COSTS OF DOWNSIZING VERSUS THE NO-LAYOFF PAYOFF[41]

In this chapter, we have touted the virtues of stability and employment security. We have highlighted companies that have instituted no-layoff policies. They recognize that massive layoffs can backfire after taking into account the costs associated with

- severance and rehiring costs,
- potential lawsuits from aggrieved workers,
- loss of institutional memory and trust in management, and
- lack of employees when the economy rebounds.

In contrast, companies that avoid employment downsizing say they get these results:

- Higher customer satisfaction
- Readiness to snap back with the economy

- A recruiting edge
- Workers who aren't afraid to innovate, knowing their jobs are safe

Remember, it's all a matter of perspective. Downsizers see employees as costs to be cut. They constantly ask, "What's the minimum number of people we need to run our business?" Responsible restructurers, on the other hand, see employees as assets to be developed. Their philosophy is "How can we use the people we already have on board more effectively?" The costs and benefits of the two approaches are clear. The choice is yours.

7

Responsible Restructuring: What to Do and What Not to Do

Even though there is no one, right way to restructure, following the guidelines presented in this chapter has yielded positive results for companies and their workforces.

Two key considerations in any restructuring effort are justice and communication. These two themes are so important that they deserve separate treatment, prior to discussing in more specific terms what to do and what not to do. Let's begin by defining some terms.

Justice refers to the maintenance or administration of what is fair, especially by the impartial adjustment of conflicting claims or the assignment of merited rewards or punishments.[1] It is one of the fundamental bases of cooperative action in organizations.[2]

Procedural justice focuses on the fairness of the procedures used to make decisions. Procedures are fair to the extent that they are consistent across persons and over time, free from bias, based on accurate information, correctable, and based on prevailing moral and ethical standards.[3]

Distributive justice focuses on the fairness of the outcomes of decisions—for example, in allocating bonuses or merit pay or in making decisions about who goes and who stays in a layoff situation. In simple terms, it is the belief that everyone should "get what they deserve."

Both procedural and distributive justice can be combined into a broader term, organizational justice.

WHY ADDRESS ORGANIZATIONAL JUSTICE?

In the wake of decisions that affect them, such as those involving pay, promotions, or layoffs, employees often ask, "Was that fair?" Judgments about the fairness or equity of procedures used to make decisions—that is, procedural justice—are rooted in the perceptions of employees. Strong research evidence indicates that such perceptions lead to important consequences, such as employee behavior and attitudes.[4] When employees feel that they have not been treated fairly, they may retaliate in the form of theft, sabotage, and even violence.[5] In short, the judgments of employees about procedural justice matter. Here is what one set of researchers had to say about fairness:[6]

> A workplace is perceived to be fair when three key elements are present: trust, openness, and respect. When an organization achieves community, people trust one another to fulfill their roles in shared projects, to communicate openly about their intentions, and to show mutual respect. When an organization acts fairly, it values every person who contributes to its success, it indicates that every individual is important. All three elements of fairness are essential to maintaining a person's engagement with work. In contrast, their absence contributes to burnout.

Procedurally fair treatment has been demonstrated to result in reduced stress[7] and increased performance, job satisfaction, commitment to an organization, and trust. It also encourages *organizational citizenship behaviors* (discretionary behaviors performed outside one's formal role that help other employees perform their jobs or that show support for and conscientiousness toward the organization).[8] As we noted in chapter 6, these include behaviors such as the following:

- Volunteering to carry out activities that are not formally a part of one's job
- Persisting with extra enthusiasm or effort when necessary to complete one's own tasks successfully
- Helping and cooperating with others

- Following organizational rules and procedures, even when they are personally inconvenient
- Endorsing, supporting, and defending organizational objectives[9]

Procedural justice affects citizenship behaviors by influencing employees' perceptions of *organizational support*, the extent to which the organization values employees' general contributions and cares for their well-being. In turn, this prompts employees to reciprocate with organizational citizenship behaviors.[10] These effects have been demonstrated to occur at the level of the work group as well as at the level of the individual.[11] In general, perceptions of procedural justice are most relevant and important to employees during times of significant organizational change. When employees experience change, their perceptions of fairness become especially potent factors that determine their attitudes and their behavior.[12] Since the only constant in organizations is change, considerations of procedural justice will always be relevant.

COMPONENTS OF PROCEDURAL JUSTICE

Although disagreement pervades the professional literature about the number of components of the broad topic of organizational justice,[13] we consider procedural justice to have three components. The first of these is *employee voice*. Organizational policies and rules may provide lots of opportunities for employee input to decisions.

The second component, known as *interactional justice*, refers to the quality of interpersonal treatment that employees receive in their everyday work. Treating others with dignity and respect is the positive side of interactional justice. Derogatory judgments, deception, invasion of privacy, inconsiderate or abusive actions, public criticism, and coercion represent the negative side of interactional justice.[14] Violating any of these elements of interactional justice leads to decreased perceptions of fair treatment. Evidence indicates that employee perceptions of interactional justice that stem from the quality of their relationships with their supervisors are positively related to their performance, citizenship behaviors directed toward their supervisors, and job satisfaction.[15]

Informational justice is the third component of procedural justice. It is expressed in terms of providing explanations or accounts for decisions made. Consider layoffs for example. Evidence indicates that layoff survivors who were provided explanations for the layoffs, or who received advance notice of them, had more positive reactions to layoffs and higher commitment to the organization.[16] Survivors had the most negative reactions to layoffs when they identified with the victims and when they perceived the layoffs to be unfair.[17]

Think about your own experiences in times of change. Was the fairness of procedures important to you? Did your perceptions affect your attitudes toward your employer and your behavior at work? Did you wish you had more say in decisions that might affect you? When it comes to restructuring, decision makers must always keep in mind that the first question employees will ask themselves, and discuss with others, is "Am I (or are we) being treated fairly?"

THE IMPORTANCE OF COMMUNICATION

Communication is undeniably important, especially during times of change. Unfortunately, this truism is often honored more in the breach than in the observance. To illustrate some of the outcomes of effective communication, consider the results of a four-month field study of communication following a merger.[18]

The study was done in two plants engaged in light manufacturing that belonged to one of two merging Fortune 500 companies. The driving force behind the merger was the belief by both CEOs that considerable strategic advantages could be created by combining complementary product lines, sharing sales and distribution for certain product lines, and eliminating functional and staff employees and facilities in a number of divisions. Clearly the merger would involve significant restructuring of operations and individuals' responsibilities.

The researchers selected two plants for study. One was located in the midwestern United States; the other was located in the Southwest. Each produced the same products and had approximately the same number of employees, management structures and systems, employment practices, and volume of output. Neither plant was unionized.

One plant—called the experimental plant—received early and frequent communication during the planning phase. The other plant—called the control plant—received no special communications. Rather, managers communicated as usual. Researchers administered a survey to employees of both plants after the announcement as well as three months later. The survey measured the perceptions of employees about the following issues: uncertainty; satisfaction; intentions to remain with the organization; stress; self-reported performance; and perceptions of the company's trustworthiness, honesty, and caring.

Communication Strategies On the day that the company released the merger announcement to the press, but before it actually reached the press, all employees of the company received a letter from the CEO informing them of the merger. The letter stated that the merger agreement had been signed and that the primary motivation was to improve the competitive position of both firms by combining complementary product lines and achieving economies of scale. The letter also stated that doing so would require the companies to share distribution and sales forces for certain products and that redundant facilities and jobs would have to be eliminated. The letter provided no specific details about individuals or work units.

In addition to the letter from the CEO, employees in the experimental plant received specific information about how the merger would affect them immediately after that information became available. Top management's intentions were to (1) provide employees with frequent, honest, and relevant information about the merger, (2) to handle employees fairly, and (3) to answer employees' questions and concerns to the fullest extent possible.

To facilitate two-way communication between management and the employees, the company used three different kinds of media to communicate with employees in the experimental plant. These were a merger newsletter, a telephone hotline, and weekly meetings among the experimental plant's manager, supervisors, and employees of each of the eight departments in the plant.

Employees in the control plant did not receive any formal communications concerning the merger other than the initial letter from the CEO. The plant manager, who was not aware of the communications program at the experimental plant, was told simply that the information would be coming as soon as it was available. This approach to communication was typical of the organization for past organizational changes.

Results   Changes in employees' perceptions from two weeks after the merger was announced to three months later were dramatic, as the following table shows:[19]

EMPLOYEE PERCEPTIONS	CONTROL PLANT	EXPERIMENTAL PLANT
Stress	9% increase	No change
Uncertainty	24% increase	2% increase
Job satisfaction	21% decrease	7% increase
Commitment	11% decrease	No change
Company is caring, trustworthy, and honest	25% decrease	14% increase
Intention to remain	12% decrease	6% decrease
Performance	20% decrease	No change

Additional Results and Implications of the Study   The changes that occurred in the two plants over time are particularly interesting. In the control plant the changes continued to be significant and negative throughout the entire study. Rather than diminishing, the problems associated with the merger continued to reverberate throughout the plant.

The situation in the experimental plant was quite different. Immediately following the merger announcement a change for the worse occurred, much as in the control plant. Once the intensive communications strategy was instituted though, the situation in the plant began to stabilize. Uncertainty and its associated outcomes did not decline, but they stopped increasing. Over time, perceptions of the company's trustworthiness, honesty, and caring, along with self-reported performance, actually began to improve and to move back toward their preannouncement levels.

These results are consistent with those in the field of organizational justice. They indicate that even people who are unhappy with the outcome of a process will have less dissatisfaction and fewer dysfunctions than they might otherwise if they understand the process through open communications and see that it was fair.[20] Open and ongoing communication is critical to a successful restructuring effort.

DEVELOPING A SYSTEMATIC COMMUNICATIONS STRATEGY

At the outset, it is important to be clear about the objectives of such a strategy and the benefits to management of implementing it. The following six points are especially important:[21]

- Obtain employee understanding and acceptance.
- Build support among all stakeholders.
- Minimize the crippling effects of uncertainty.
- Keep people focused, energized, and committed to the organization.
- Change employee behavior as required.
- Sustain organizational performance.

It is important to recognize that employees will be unusually confused and worried in the midst of the changes that are brewing. Uncertainty is punishing to them, and rumors flourish. Even minor events may be imbued with great meaning. Simple mistakes become sinister plots. Unrelated events become causal links. Absent real information, employees fill in the blanks with their own information—and the answers they create are invariably far worse than the reality that awaits them.[22]

When communication is inadequate, employees don't trust what they are told and they do not understand the need or reasons for change. They don't understand what is required of them, and they spend an inordinate amount of time looking after "number 1."

What Not to Do

Don't overrely on communications that are not face-to-face, such as e-mail, intranet, memoranda, or newsletters. Don't use exclusively one-way (downward) approaches, with no listening to find out what is important to employees and managers. Such approaches are known as "tell and sell." Don't just communicate platitudes and hype (e.g., "We're doing this to become more competitive").

Finally, don't get the source wrong. For major announcements, use the CEO, not the immediate supervisor. Employees want clear signals about the future from the CEO, and here are some guidelines on how to proceed.

What the CEO Must Do[23]

First, silence is *not* an option, even if you don't have all the answers. In planning your communications strategy, you have to know the issues that are most important to the firm's stakeholders (e.g., employees, suppliers, customers, and local communities) so that you can address those issues. Then you must speak to them through channels they trust, in terms that they understand.

In developing an integrated information strategy, there are four firm rules. We might call them "The Four No's." There should be no secrets, no surprises, no hype, and no empty promises. As CEO, you must be very well prepared. More specifically, your role is to ensure that

- the "story" is true, consistent, and will work;
- the vision is clear, even if details are not;
- managers and supervisors are in the loop; and
- support materials are available and tested.

In addition, make sure that most primary communication is face-to-face. Supplement presentations to large groups (e.g., in an auditorium or via closed-circuit television or satellite) with small-group meetings with employees, managers, and other stakeholders. Depending on the size of your organization and the numbers of people involved, a "small group" could include as many as 40 people. Small-group meetings allow the CEO to engage in real dialogue, where he or she can listen and learn from participants, as well as share information informally.

IMPLEMENTING A CORPORATE COMMUNICATION EFFORT[24]

Here are some guidelines for communicating information about a company's restructuring initiatives.

- **Develop a detailed plan**. It should include various phases, such as initial announcement by the CEO, followed by briefings for executives, middle managers, and first-level supervisors. In turn, they will meet with their direct reports to convey more detailed information. Announcements and

briefings will be supplemented with written materials is-
sued on a regular basis, such as newsletters, e-mails, and
regular updates on the company's intranet. Identify the key
factors necessary for success at each stage, and be able to
put the overall plan on a single page.

- **Build a new communication system**. Restructuring creates
  a turbulent environment. Recognize that it is not "business
  as usual." Create a communication team and network to
  drive the overall effort. Provide coaching and counseling
  to all communicators to ensure that they are capable. Ensure that accountabilities are clear. Most importantly, create new media with a sunset clause (i.e., a specified time
  for discontinuance). The media might include an intranet
  site, e-mails, written and electronic bulletins, and special
  briefings.

- **Lock in executive support**. Explain to executives exactly
  what the issues are for each group of stakeholders. Alternate between the overall objectives of the communication
  strategy and the details of the communications plan until
  they are comfortable with both. Strive for common understanding, so that everyone is "on the same page."

- **Develop your "story."** Explain who, what, why, where, and
  how. The story must be true, based on facts rather than
  speculation, and it must be consistent across all spokesper-
  sons. After the initial announcement from the CEO, don't
  delay in getting out "the rest of the story." Move fast. Be
  sure your communications are consistent, constant, and,
  above all, uncomplicated. As has often been said, there is
  elegance in simplicity.

- **Listen, listen, listen**. Constantly gather "intelligence" from
  front-line employees, managers, and other stakeholders.
  Solicit their reactions to what they have been told. Ask
  them what they don't understand. Take another look at
  your communications content and strategy, and refine it
  as necessary to address stakeholders' concerns.

- **Assess communications and performance**. Do people know
  what is going on? Do they understand the implications of
  the restructuring effort for themselves, for their teams, for
  their part of the business, and for the organization as a

whole? Assess key performance indicators such as sales, lost time, and quality to gauge the impact of the communications on performance.

- **Keep the plan current**. Use the communication team and network to review the detailed communication plan morning and night. Update it constantly to address new developments or as information becomes known. Do not assume anything.

Having examined the crucial roles of organizational justice and organizational communications, let's consider some key things to avoid.

10 MISTAKES TO AVOID WHEN RESTRUCTURING[25]

1. **Failing to be clear about long- and short-term goals.** Always ask, "What do our customers expect from us, how can we best serve them, and how will restructuring affect our ability to meet those expectations and service requirements?"

2. **Using downsizing as a first resort, rather than as a last resort**. In some cases, firms downsize because they see competitors doing it. This is a "cloning" response, in which executives in different firms follow one another's actions under conditions of uncertainty,[26] but it fails to consider alternative approaches to reducing costs.

3. **Using nonselective downsizing**. Across-the-board job cuts miss the mark. So also do cuts based on criteria such as last-in-first-out (because then firms lose all their bright young people), removal of everyone below a certain level in the hierarchy (because top-heavy firms become even top heavier), or the weeding out of all middle managers (because firms lose a wealth of experience and connections).[27] Are all departments and all employees equally valuable to the firm? Probably not. With respect to employees, think about performance and replaceability. Employees who are top performers, who work well together, and who are diffi-

cult to replace are most valuable. This is the reservoir of talent that firms will depend on to innovate, to create new markets and new customers. Do everything you can to retain that talent.

4. **Failing to change the way work is done**. Some firms assume that cutting perks is a cure-all for other problems and that they can keep making products or delivering services the same way as before downsizing.[28] They fail even to consider changing from an old way to a new way of working. The same amount of work is loaded on the backs of fewer workers.

5. **Failing to involve workers in the restructuring process**. It is a truism that employees are more likely to support what they helped create, yet many restructuring efforts fail to involve employees in any decisions about either the process or the desired outcomes. As a result, employees feel powerless and helpless, and massive uncertainty invades the organization. Conversely, when employees were asked to rate various factors that affect attracting, motivating, and retaining superior employees, one of the most important factors was "opportunities to participate in decisions."[29]

6. **Failing to communicate openly and honestly**. Don't allow employees to hear about cutbacks through the grapevine. We noted earlier that failure to provide regular, ongoing updates not only contributes to the atmosphere of uncertainty but also does nothing to dispel rumors. Open, honest communication is crucial if employees are to trust what management says, and trust is crucial to successful restructuring.[30] People trust leaders who make themselves known and make their positions clear.[31]

7. **Handling ineptly those who lose their jobs.** Failure to treat departing employees with dignity and respect (e.g., having security guards escort them off company property), failure to provide training to supervisors in how to handle emotional factors, and failure to provide assistance to departing employees (financial, counseling, redeployment, training, outplacement) comprise another crucial mistake.[32]

8. **Failing to manage survivors effectively**. Employee morale is often the first casualty of downsizing, as survivors become

narrow-minded, self-absorbed, and risk-averse.[33] Many firms underestimate the emotional damage that survivors suffer by watching others lose their jobs. In fact, a great deal of research shows that survivors often suffer from heightened levels of stress, burnout, uncertainty about their own roles in the new organization, and an overall sense of betrayal.[34] In unionized environments, downsizing may be related to increased grievances, higher absenteeism rates, workplace conflict, and poorer supervisor-union member relations.[35] In fact, survivors are looking for signals such as the following: Were departing employees treated fairly, and with dignity and respect? Why should I stay? What new opportunities will be available to me if I choose to do so? Is there a new business strategy to help us do a better job of competing in the marketplace?

9. **Ignoring the effects on other stakeholders**. In addition to survivors and victims, it is important to think through the potential consequences of restructuring on customers, suppliers, shareholders, and the local community. A comprehensive program addresses and manages consequences to each of these groups.

10. **Failing to evaluate results and learn from mistakes**. Restructuring is not a one-time event for most firms. Unless firms are brutally honest about the processes and outcomes of their restructuring efforts, they are doomed to repeat the same mistakes over and over again. Don't be afraid to ask employees and managers at all levels, "What did you like most and like least about our restructuring effort?" Don't be afraid to ask customers whether the firm is now meeting their needs more effectively, and for suggestions on how it might do so.

Now that we have seen what so many firms do wrong, let's examine how to do it right.

RESTRUCTURING RESPONSIBLY: WHAT TO DO[36]

At this point you are probably wondering how to proceed. We have provided examples of strategies for restructuring responsibly and highlighted some things not to do. Put it all together by following these suggestions:

1. **Build a plan for restructuring into the overall economic plan for your business.** Recognize that in the course of developing your organization over the long term, there will be economic swings both up and down, as well as changes in the course of business and in technology. "Preventive planning" is a key difference between organizations that can deal with such changes in a systematic, orderly way, versus those that resort to knee-jerk reactions to respond swiftly (often through mass layoffs). Companies like Reflexite and Southwest Airlines are good examples of preventive planners.

2. **Carefully consider the rationale behind restructuring.** Invest in analysis and consider the impact on those who stay, those who leave, and the ability of the organization to serve its customers. Do you have a long-term strategic plan that identifies the future mission and vision of the organization, as well as its core competencies? Does the plan consider how processes can be redesigned while retaining the high performers who will be crucial to the firm's future success? Is there a plan to sell off unprofitable assets? Is downsizing part of a plan or is it *the* plan?

3. **Consider the virtues of stability.** As we saw in chapter 6, many benefits are associated with a no-layoff pledge. In many cases, companies can maintain their special efficiencies only if they can give their workers a unique set of skills and a feeling that they belong together. Teams work best if the team members get to know and trust each other, and if each team member masters a broad enough range of skills to be able to fill in for absent colleagues. Moreover, profit sharing as a reward system makes sense only if the employees are around when profits are disbursed. Sometimes the virtues of stability outweigh the potential benefits of change.

4. **Before making any final decisions about restructuring, managers should make their concerns known to employees and seek their input.** As chapter 5 illustrated, sometimes workers have insightful ideas that may make layoffs unnecessary. However, even if layoffs are necessary, seeking

employee input will foster a sense of participation, belonging, and personal control. To be sure, seeking input from
knowledgeable employees in decisions that affect them
should be a regular part of managing, but it is even more
important to do so in times of significant organizational
change. Make special efforts to secure the input of "star"
employees or opinion leaders, for they can help communicate the rationale and strategy of restructuring to their fellow employees and also help promote trust in the
restructuring effort.

5. **Don't use downsizing as a "quick fix" to achieve short-
term goals in the face of long-term problems**. Consider
other alternatives first, and ensure that management at
all levels shares the pain and participates in any sacrifices
employees are asked to bear. Like Agilent and Charles
Schwab, make downsizing truly a last resort, not a first
resort.

6. **Get lean without being mean**. When costs need to be cut,
perquisites (perks), such as free coffee, snacks, and con-
cierge services for employees are often the first to go. Often
companies slash them arbitrarily and by fiat, with little or
no chance for employee input. This is a mistake. At the
outset, explain the cutbacks in a business context that is
understandable. Let employees know what the numbers
add up to. Ask employees which perks are most important to them. For example, matching funds in company-
sponsored savings plans such as 401(k), medical/dental insurance, day care, and flextime are usually "untouchable"
from the employees' perspective. Try to scale back perks
without eliminating them entirely. Thus, Aetna is saving
$400,000 a year by making employees at its Bluebell,
Pennsylvania, office buy their own coffee and tea.

7. **If layoffs are necessary, be sure that the process of selecting
excess positions is perceived as fair and that decisions are
made in a consistent manner**. Make special efforts to retain
the best and the brightest, and provide maximum advance
notice to terminated employees.

8. **Communicate regularly and in a variety of ways to keep
everyone abreast of new developments and information**.
As we noted earlier, use newsletters, e-mails, videos, and

employee meetings for this purpose. Sharing confidential financial and competitive information with employees establishes a climate of trust and honesty. High-level managers should be visible, active participants in this process, and be sure lower-level managers are trained to address the concerns of victims as well as survivors.

9. **Give survivors a reason to stay and prospective new hires a reason to join.** As one set of authors noted, "People need to believe in the organization to make it work, but they need to see that it works to believe in it."[37] Recognize that surviving employees ultimately are the people you will depend on to provide the innovation, superior service to customers, and healthy corporate culture that will attract and retain top talent. Do everything you can to ensure their commitment and their trust.

10. **Train employees and their managers in the new ways of operating.** Restructuring means change, and employees at all levels need help in coping with changes in areas such as reporting relationships, new organizational arrangements, and reengineered business processes. Evidence indicates clearly that firms whose training budgets increase following a restructuring are more likely to realize improved productivity, profits, and quality.[38]

11. **Examine carefully all HR systems in light of the change of strategy or environment facing the firm.** Training employees in the new ways of operating is important, but so also are other HR systems. These include workforce planning, based on changes in business strategy, markets, customers, and expected economic conditions; recruitment and selection, based on the need to change both the number and skills mix of new hires; performance appraisal, based on changes in the work to be done; compensation, based on changes in skills requirements or responsibilities; and labor relations, based on the need to involve employees and their unions in the restructuring process.

Above all, if you do choose to restructure, do it responsibly, and use it as an opportunity to focus ever more sharply on those areas of the business where your firm enjoys its greatest competitive strengths. If you are willing to adjust your perspective so that you see your employees as assets to be developed rather than only as costs to be cut, you will enjoy several advantages. First, you will take a longer-term view of employment relationships and be less likely to turn to layoffs at the first sign of trouble. Second, you will see the link between management behavior that respects people at every level, acts with integrity, and demonstrates ethical decision making and the three emblems of organizational success.[39] We might call these the Three Cs: *c*are of customers, *c*onstant innovation, and *c*ommitted people.

Endnotes

CHAPTER 1

1. "The High Cost of Merrill's Cuts," *Business Week*, January 21, 2002, 40. See also "Shaking Up Merrill," *Business Week*, November 12, 2001, 96–104.
2. "Will Investors Pay for Schwab's Advice?" *Business Week*, January 21, 2002, 36. See also F. Vogelstein, "Can Schwab Get Its Mojo Back?" *Fortune*, September 17, 2001, 93–98.
3. "The Top 25 Managers," *Business Week*, January 14, 2002, 57.
4. S. Vranica, "Salary Cuts, Not Layoffs, Prevail as Hedge against Market Slump," *Wall Street Journal*, January 8, 2002, B8.
5. D. Michaels, "Airbus Chief Says Company Won't Cut Jobs," *Wall Street Journal*, January 18, 2002, A6, A8.
6. "Making Hay While It Rains," *Business Week*, January 14, 2002, 32, 33.
7. "Shaking Up Merrill," *Business Week*, November 12, 2001, 96–104.
8. W. McKinley, J. Zhao, and K. G. Rust, "A Sociocognitive Interpretation of Organizational Downsizing," *Academy of Management Review* 25 (2000): 227–243. See also F. Ostroff, *The Horizontal Organization* (New York: Oxford University Press, 1999). See also R. M. Tomasko, *Rethinking the Corporation* (New York: AMACOM, 1993).
9. R. L. DeWitt, "Firm, Industry, and Strategy Influences on Choice of Downsizing Approach," *Strategic Management Journal* 19 (1998): 59–79.
10. S. J. Freeman and K. S. Cameron, "Organizational Downsizing: A Convergence and Reorganization Framework," *Organization Science* 4 (1993): 10–29.
11. Company press release, October 12, 2001; available at www.Polaroid.com; retrieved November 27, 2001.
12. U.S. Department of Labor, Office of the American Workplace, *Guide to Responsible Restructuring* (Washington, D.C.: U.S. Government Printing Office, 1995); available at www.dol.gov/dol/oaw/public/non-regs/publications/respres.htm#about.
13. The source for material in this section is W. F. Cascio, "Strategies for Responsible Restructuring," *Academy of Management Executive*, in press.
14. "Shadow of Recession"; available at www.cbsmarketwatch.com; retrieved February 9, 2002.

15. Sources: ibid. See also "Terror's Aftermath: Layoffs," *Business Week*, October 8, 2001, 10; B. Hale, "Always Look on the Bright Side of a Severe Recession," *Sydney Morning Herald*, November 5, 2001, 38; J. C. Cooper and K. Madigan, "The Bad News on Unemployment Will Only Get Worse," *Business Week*, November 19, 2001, 31; J. Shiver Jr., "American Workers Rip Visa Program," *Denver Post*, November 22, 2001, 2A; J. Clout, "Battered Merrill's Income Halved," *Financial Review*, October 22, 2001, 1.

16. B. Morris, "White-Collar Blues," *Fortune*, July 23, 2201, 98–110.

17. "CEO Shakeout," *Business Week*, November 12, 2001, 14.

18. "Savaged by the Slowdown," *Business Week*, September 17, 2001, 75.

19. Ibid.

20. A. Barrionuevo, "Jobless in a Flash, Enron's Ex-employees Are Stunned, Bitter, Ashamed," *Wall Street Journal*, December 11, 2001, B1, B12.

21. Ibid., 74–77. See also "Snip, Snip, Oops!" *The Economist*, October 13, 2001, 59, 60.

22. C. Maslach and M. P. Leiter, *The Truth about Burnout: How Organizations Cause Personal Stress and What to Do about It* (San Francisco: Jossey-Bass, 1997), 23.

23. Ibid.

24. "Downsized in a Down Economy," *Business Week*, September 17, 2001, 36.

25. T. Horwitz, "Home Alone 2: Some Who Lost Jobs in Early '90s Recession Find a Hard Road Back," *Wall Street Journal*, June 26, 1998, A1, A9.

26. J. A. Colquitt, D. E. Conlon, M. J. Wesson, C. O. L. H. Porter, and K. Y. Ng, "Justice at the Millennium: A Meta-analytic Review of 25 Years of Organizational Justice Research," *Journal of Applied Psychology* 86 (2001): 425–445. See also F. Fehr and S. Gächter, "Fairness and Retaliation," *Journal of Economic Perspectives* 14, no. 3 (2000): 159–182.

27. A. B. Krueger and A. Mas, *Strikes, Scabs, and Tread Separations: Labor Strife and the Production of Defective Bridgestone/Firestone Tires*; available at www.irs.princeton.edu; retrieved January 11, 2002.

28. D. Wessel, "The Hidden Cost of Labor Strife," *Wall Street Journal*, January 10, 2002, A1.

29. A. Forrest, "The Bottom Line," *South China Morning Post, Sunday Money*, February 10, 2002, 5.

30. M. Bennett, Hewitt Associates, "Best Employers in Asia," paper presented at the National Manpower Summit, Singapore, October 18, 2001.

31. "America's Most Admired Companies," 2001; available at www.Fortune.com; retrieved February 8, 2002.

32. N. Stein, "Global Most Admired: Measuring People Power," October 2, 2000; available at www.Fortune.com; retrieved February 10, 2002.

33. C. D'Andrea, "Wall Street and Work Life," unpublished manuscript, Bright Horizons Family Solutions, Port Washington, NY.

CHAPTER 2

1. R. J. Bos and M. Ruotolo, *General Criteria for S&P U. S. Index Membership,* September 2000; available at www.standardandpoors.com; retrieved February 9, 2002.
2. W. F. Cascio, C. E. Young, and J. R. Morris, "Financial Consequences of Employment-Change Decisions in Major U. S. Corporations," *Academy of Management Journal* 40, no. 5 (1997): 1175–1189. See also J. R. Morris, W. F. Cascio, and C. E. Young, "Have Employment Downsizings Been Successful?" *Organizational Dynamics* (Winter 1999): 78–87.
3. Morris et al., op. cit., 85.
4. V. B. Wayhan and S. Werner, "The Impact of Workforce Reductions on Financial Performance: A Longitudinal Perspective," *Journal of Management* 26 (2000): 341–363. See also K. P. DeMeuse, T. J. Bergmann, and P. A. Vanderheiden, "Corporate Downsizing: Separating Myth from Fact," *Journal of Management Inquiry* 6 (1997): 168–176.
5. J. Collins, *Good to Great: Why Some Companies Make the Leap and Others Don't* (New York: Harper Business, 2001).
6. W. F. Cascio and C. E. Young, "Financial Consequences of Employment-Change Decisions in Major U. S. Corporations: 1982–2000," in *Resizing the Organization,* ed. K. P. De Meuse and M. L. Marks (San Francisco: Jossey-Bass, in press).
7. Cascio et al., op. cit.
8. J. Welch with J. A. Byrne, *Jack: Straight from the Gut* (New York: Warner Business Books, 2001).
9. W. F. Cascio, "Downsizing: What Do We Know? What Have We Learned?" *Academy of Management Executive* 7, no. 1 (1993): 95–104. See also W. F. Cascio, "Strategies for Responsible Restructuring," keynote address presented at the National Manpower Summit, Singapore, October 2001.

CHAPTER 3

1. B. Morris, "White-Collar Blues," *Fortune,* July 23, 2001, 98–110. For material in myths 1, 2, 8, and 9, see also W. F. Cascio, "Strategies for Responsible Restructuring," *Academy of Management Executive,* in press.
2. C. Ansberry, "Private Resources: By Resisting Layoffs, Small Manufacturers Help Protect Economy," *Wall Street Journal,* July 6, 2001, A1, A2.
3. S. Armour, "Companies Hire Even as They Lay Off," *USA Today,* June 24–26, 2001, 1.
4. American Management Association, *2000 American Management Association Survey: Staffing and Structure* (New York: Author, 2000). See also "Hire Math: Fire 3, Add 5," *Business Week,* March 13, 2000, 28.

5. Society for Human Resource Management, *2001 Layoffs and Job Security Survey* (Alexandria, VA: Author, 2001); available at www.shrm.org/surveys/results.
6. L. Uchitelle, "Pink Slip? Now, It's All in a Day's Work," *New York Times*, August 5, 2001; available at www.NYTimes.com; retrieved September 24, 2001.
7. W. F. Cascio and C. E. Young, "Financial Consequences of Employment-Change Decisions in Major U. S. Corporations: 1982–2000," in *Resizing the Organization*, ed. K. De Meuse and M. L. Marks (San Francisco: Jossey-Bass, in press).
8. Society for Human Resource Management, op. cit.
9. E. Quinones, "Massive Staff Cutbacks No Guarantee of Profits," *Denver Post*, February 9, 1998, 3C.
10. These data were reported in R. Cravotta and B. H. Kleiner, "New Developments Concerning Reductions in Force," *Management Research News* 24, no. 3/4 (2001): 90–93.
11. "Why Pink Slips Don't Necessarily Add Up to Productivity Hikes," *Business Week*, July 4, 1994, 20.
12. American Management Association, "Corporate Downsizing, Job Elimination, and Job Creation: Summary of Key Findings," in *1996 AMA Survey* (New York: Author, 1996), 1–11.
13. U.S. Department of Labor, Office of the American Workplace, *Guide to Responsible Restructuring* (Washington, D.C.: U.S. Government Printing Office, 1995); available at www.dol.gov/dol/oaw/public/nonregs/publications/respres.htmabout. See also Quinones, op. cit.
14. Society for Human Resource Management, op. cit.
15. S. H. Appelbaum, A. Everard, and L. T. S. Hung, "Strategic Downsizing: Critical Success Factors," *Management Decision* 37, no. 7 (1999): 535–552. See also H. Mirvis, "Human Resource Management: Leaders, Laggards, and Followers," *Academy of Management Executive* 11, no. 2 (1997): 43–56; M. F. R. Kets de Vries and K. Balazs, "The Downside of Downsizing," *Human Relations* 50, no. 1 (1997): 11–50.
16. "Too Much Work, Too Little Time," *Business Week*, July 16, 2001, 12.
17. R. Gittins, "Survivors of Downsizing Count the Cost," *Sydney Morning Herald*, August 1, 2001, 12.
18. Uchitelle, op. cit.
19. "The Year Downsizing Grew Up," *The Economist*, December 21, 1996, 97–100.
20. S. R. Fisher and M. A. White, "Downsizing in a Learning Organization: Are There Hidden Costs?" *Academy of Management Review* 25 (2000): 244–251.
21. J. H. Neuman and R. A. Baron, "Workplace Violence and Workplace Aggression: Evidence Concerning Specific Forms, Potential Causes, and Preferred Targets," *Journal of Management* 24 (1998): 391–419.

See also J. Burlingame, "Layoff Methodologies: Downsizing with Grace," *Trajectory Magazine* (October 2001): 1.

22. "After the Shooting Stops," *Business Week*, March 12, 2001, 98–100.

23. Neuman and Baron, op. cit. See also J. T. Adams III, "Workplace Deaths Decline, Coworker Homicides Rise," *HRMagazine* (February 2001): 12.

24. J. Carreyrou, "In France, Labor Resorts to Radical Tactics," *Wall Street Journal*, November 19, 2001, A13. See also C. Matlack, "The High Cost of France's Aversion to Layoffs," *Business Week*, November 5, 2001, 56.

25. "Revenge of the Downsized Nerds," *Business Week*, July 30, 2001, 40.

26. American Management Association, op. cit.

27. Northwestern National Life, *Employee Burnout: America's Newest Epidemic (Minneapolis: Author, 1991)*.

28. M. E. Cohen, "Downsizing and Disability Go Together," *Business and Health* 15, no. 1 (1997): 10. See also S. H. Applebaum, S. Lavigne-Schmidt, M. Peytchev, and B. Shapiro, "Downsizing: Measuring the Costs of Failure," *Journal of Management Development* 18, no. 5 (1999): 436–463.

29. Kets de Vries and Balazs, op. cit. See also C. R. Leana, D. C. Feldman, and G. Y. Tan, "Predictors of Coping Behavior after a Layoff," *Journal of Organizational Behavior* 19, no. 1 (1998): 85–97; C. R. Leana and D. C. Feldman, *Coping with Job Loss: How Individuals, Organizations, and Communities Respond to Layoffs* (New York: Macmillan/Lexington, 1992).

30. M. Clarke and M. Patrickson, "Does Downsized Mean Down and Out?" *Asia Pacific Journal of Human Resources* 39, no. 1 (2001): 63–78.

31. Leana and Feldman, op. cit.

32. J. C. Latack and J. B. Dozier, "After the Ax Falls: Job Loss as a Career Transition," *Academy of Management Review* 11, no. 2 (1986): 376. See also C. Maslach and M. Leiter, *The Truth about Burnout: How Organizations Cause Personal Stress and What to Do about It* (San Francisco: Jossey-Bass, 1997), 42–44.

33. Clarke and Patrickson, op. cit.

CHAPTER 4

1. J. Pfeffer, *The Human Equation: Building Profits by Putting People First* (Boston: Harvard Business School Press, 1998); D. E. Terpstra and E. J. Rozell, "The Relationship of Staffing Practices to Organizational-Level Measures of Performance," *Personnel Psychology* 46 (1993): 27–48. See also B. Gerhart and G. T. Milkovich, "Organizational Differences in Managerial Compensation and Firm Performance," *Academy of Management Journal* 33 (1990): 663–691.

2. Pfeffer, op. cit. See also J. Bae and J. J. Lawler, "Organizational and HRM Strategies in Korea: Impact on Firm Performance in an Emerging Economy," *Academy of Management Journal* 43 (2000): 502–517; G. R. Ferris, W. A. Hochwarter, M. R. Buckley, G. Harrell-Cook, and D. Frink, "Human Resources Management: Some New Directions," *Journal of Management* 25 (1999): 385–415; J. E. Delery and D. H. Doty, "Modes of Theorizing in Strategic Human Resource Management: Tests of Universalistic, Contingency, and Configurational Performance Predictions," *Academy of Management Journal* 39 (1996): 802–835.

3. A. S. Tsui, J. L. Pearce, L. W. Porter, and A. M. Tripoli, "Alternative Approaches to the Employee–Organization Relationship: Does Investment in Employees Pay Off?" *Academy of Management Journal* 40, no. 5 (1997): 1089–1121.

4. See, for example, E. E. Lawler III, *The Ultimate Advantage: Creating the High-Involvement Organization* (San Francisco: Jossey-Bass, 1992). See also J. B. Arthur, "Effects of Human Resource Systems on Manufacturing Performance and Turnover," *Academy of Management Journal* 37 (1994): 670–687; J. B. Arthur, "The Link between Business Strategy and Industrial Relations Systems in American Steel Minimills," *Industrial and Labor Relations Review* 45 (1992): 488–506.

5. Tsui et al., op. cit.

6. J. P. MacDuffie and J. Krafcik, "Integrating Technology and Human Resources for High-Performance Manufacturing," in *Transforming Organizations*, ed. T. Kochan and M. Useem (New York: Oxford University Press, 1992), 210–226.

7. T. M. Welbourne and A. O. Andrews, "Predicting the Performance of Initial Public Offerings: Should Human Resource Management Be in the Equation?" *Academy of Management Journal* 39 (1996): 891–919.

8. W. N. Davidson III, D. L. Worrell, and J. B. Fox, "Early Retirement Programs and Firm Performance," *Academy of Management Journal* 39 (1996): 970–984.

9. M. A. Huselid and B. E. Becker, "The Impact of High Performance Work Systems, Implementation Effectiveness, and Alignment with Strategy on Shareholder Wealth," unpublished paper, Rutgers University, 1997, 18–19. See also M. A. Huselid, "The Impact of Human Resource Management Practices on Turnover, Productivity, and Corporate Financial Performance," *Academy of Management Journal* 38 (1995): 635–672.

10. A. M. Ryan, M. J. Schmit, and R. Johnson, "Attitudes and Effectiveness: Examining Relations at an Organizational Level," *Personnel Psychology* 49 (1996): 853–883. See also A. Cohen, "Organizational Commitment and Turnover: A Meta-analysis," *Academy of Management Journal* 36 (1993): 1140–1157; and C. Ostroff, "The Relationship between Satisfaction, Attitudes, and Performance: An Organizational-Level Analysis," *Journal of Applied Psychology* 77 (1992): 963–974.

11. A. J. Rucci, S. P. Kirn, and R. T. Quinn, "The Employee-Customer-Profit Chain at Sears," *Harvard Business Review* (January–February 1998) 82–97.
12. B. E. Becker, M. A. Huselid, and D. Ulrich, *The HR Scorecard* (Boston: Harvard Business School Press, 2001).
13. Ibid., 18.
14. G. Hamel, *Leading the Revolution* (Boston: Harvard Business School Press, 2001).
15. Retrieved from the World Wide Web at www.Fortune.com on February 6, 2002.
16. F. Norris, "Financial Magic Looked Good, but Left Companies Weak," *New York Times,* September 28, 2001; available at www.NYTimes.com; retrieved September 28, 2001.
17. T. A. Stewart, *Intellectual Capital: The New Wealth of Organizations* (New York: Doubleday/Currency, 1997).

CHAPTER 5
1. F. Vogelstein, "Can Schwab Get Its Mojo Back?" *Fortune,* September 17, 2001, 93–98. See also A. Bernstein, "America's Future: The Human Factor," *Business Week,* August 27, 2001, 118–122. For material on Schwab, Cisco, and Philips Electronics, see also W. F. Cascio, "Strategies for Responsible Restructuring," *Academy of Management Executive,* in press.
2. M. Boyle, "How to Cut Perks without Killing Morale," *Fortune,* February 19, 2001, 241, 242, 244.
3. F. Jossi, "Laying Off Well," *HRMagazine* (July 2001): 48.
4. S. Caudron, "Teach Downsizing Survivors How to Thrive," *Personnel Journal* (January 1996): 38–48.
5. "Where's the Upside?" *Business Week,* September 17, 2001, 40–43.
6. Ibid. See also S. Lohr, "Suit against Hewlett Deal Is Dismissed," *New York Times,* May 1, 2002, available at www.nytimes.com, retrieved May 1, 2002; M. Williams, "Compaq Beauty Differs in Eyes of H-P Holders," *Wall Street Journal,* December 3, 2001, B7.
7. Bernstein, op. cit.
8. L. Uchitelle, "Pink Slip? Now, It's All in a Day's Work," *New York Times,* August 5, 2001; available at www.NYTimes.com; retrieved September 24, 2001.
9. "The Best 100 Companies to Work For," *Fortune,* February 4, 2002, 73.
10. Bernstein, op. cit.
11. Uchitelle, op. cit.
12. "State Program to Help Firms Avoid Lay-offs: Companies Cut Hours Instead of Employees," *New London Day,* October 21, 2001; available at Theday.com; retrieved October 23, 2001.
13. Available at www.Reflexite.com; retrieved December 4, 2001.
14. D. Edgar, Reflexite Corporation, personal communication, March 8, 1995.

15. L. Casey, Reflexite Corporation, Human Resources Department, personal communication, December 7, 2001.
16. J. Pfeffer, *The Human Equation: Building Profits by Putting People First* (Boston: Harvard Business School Press, 1998).
17. Ibid.
18. M. Robinson, Intel's manager of corporate redeployment, personal communication plus briefing materials, March 1995.
19. "The Best 100 Companies to Work For," 84.
20. J. Vitiello, *Technical and Skills Training* (Alexandria, VA: American Society for Training and Development, 1994).
21. J. Stuller, "Why Not 'Inplacement'?" *Training* (June 1993): 37–41.
22. R. Lindstad, quoted in "When Lay-offs Alone Don't Turn the Tide," *Business Week*, December 7, 1992, 100–101.
23. J. S. Lublin, "Amid Downturn, More Companies Cut Pay, Benefits," *Wall Street Journal*, December 4, 2001, B1, B12.
24. J. C. Latack and J. B. Dozier, "After the Ax Falls: Job Loss as a Career Transition," *Academy of Management Review* 11, no. 2 (1986): 375–392.
25. F. Jossi, "Take the Road Less Traveled," *HRMagazine* (July 2001): 46–51.
26. Ibid.
27. Lublin, op. cit.
28. D. Roth, "How to Cut Pay, Lay Off 8,000 People, and Still Have Workers Who Love You," *Fortune*, February 4, 2002, 62–68.
29. B. C. Dawson, quoted in Jossi, op. cit., 48.
30. D. Rigby, quoted in Jossi, op. cit., 49.
31. T. Colter, quoted in J. Carlton, "Louisiana-Pacific Workers Cut Costs to Save Their Jobs," *Wall Street Journal*, January 29, 2001, B10.
32. W. Wirfs, quoted in ibid., B10.
33. Singapore Ministry of Manpower, *Managing Excess Manpower*, Case Study Series (Singapore: Author, February 2001).
34. E. Nelson, "Job-Cut Buyouts Favored by P&G Pose Problems," *Wall Street Journal*, June 12, 2001, B1, B10.
35. D. Antoine, quoted in Nelson, op. cit., B10.

CHAPTER 6

1. R. Levering and M. Moskowitz, "The Best in the Worst of Times," *Fortune*, February 4, 2002, 60.
2. "The 100 Best Companies to Work For," *Fortune*, February 4, 2002, 82.
3. R. Cravotta and B. H. Kleiner, "New Developments Concerning Reductions in Force," *Management Research News* 24, nos. 3/4 (2001): 90–93.
4. Ibid.
5. D. W. Organ, *Organizational Citizenship Behavior: The Good Soldier Syndrome* (Lexington, MA: Lexington Books, 1988).

6. E. W. Morrison, "Role Definition and Organizational Citizenship Behavior: The Importance of the Employee's Perspective," *Academy of Management Journal* 37 (1994): 1543–1567.

7. See, for example, R. H. Moorman, G. L. Blakely, and B. Niehoff, "Does Perceived Organizational Support Mediate the Relationship between Procedural Justice and Organizational Citizenship Behavior?" *Academy of Management Journal* 41, no. 3 (1998): 351–357.

8. D. W. Organ and K. Ryan, "A Meta-analytic Review of Attitudinal and Dispositional Predictors of Organizational Citizenship Behavior," *Personnel Psychology 48* (1995): 775–802. See also T. D. Allen and M. C. Rush, "The Effects of Organizational Citizenship Behavior on Performance Judgments: A Field Study and a Laboratory Experiment," *Journal of Applied Psychology* 83 (1998): 247–260. See also M. Podsakoff and S. B. MacKenzie, "Organizational Citizenship Behaviors and Sales Unit Effectiveness," *Journal of Marketing Research* 31, no. 3 (1994): 351–363. For a brief summary of research on OCBs, see F. Luthans, *Organizational Behavior,* 9th ed. (Burr Ridge, IL: McGraw-Hill/Irwin, 2002), 238.

9. "Is Boeing Cutting Too Close to the Bone?" *Business Week,* November 26, 2001, 108, 109.

10. M. Conlin, "Where Layoffs Are a Last Resort," *Business Week Online,* October 8, 2001; available at www.businessweek.com; retrieved October 13, 2001.

11. F. Reichheld, quoted in "Snip, Snip, Oops!" *The Economist,* October 13, 2001, 59, 60.

12. F. Jossi, "Take the Road Less Traveled," *HRMagazine* (July 2001): 46–51; "A Model Incentive Plan Gets Caught in a Vise," *Business Week,* January 22, 1996, 89, 92; C. Wiley, "Incentive Plan Pushes Production," *Personnel Journal* (August 1993): 86–91; W. Serrin, "The Way That Works at Lincoln," *New York Times,* January 15, 1984, D1.

13. R. Vogt, quoted in Jossi, op. cit., 51.

14. C. Fishman, "Sanity, Inc.," *Fast Company* (January 1999): 87.

15. C. A. O'Reilly III and J. Pfeffer, "The SAS Institute: Succeeding with Old-fashioned Values in a New Industry," in C. A. O'Reilly and J. Pfeffer, *Hidden Value: How Great Companies Achieve Extraordinary Results with Ordinary People* (Boston: Harvard Business School Press, 2000), 99–120; J. Pfeffer, *SAS Institute: A Different Approach to Incentives and People Management Practices in the Software Industry* (Palo Alto: CA: Graduate School of Business, Stanford University, 2998), case HR-6.

16. See, for example, R. Lane, "Pampering the Customers, Pampering the Employees," *Forbes* (October 1996): 73–78; see also P. Cappelli, "A Market-Driven Approach to Retaining Talent," *Harvard Business Review* (January–February 2000): 103–111.

17. http://www.sas.com/corporate/report00/ar fact figures./html; retrieved December 7, 2001.

18. Fishman, op. cit.

19. Pfeffer, op. cit., 5.

20. O'Reilly and Pfeffer, op. cit., 107, 108.

21. J. Dornan, "SAS Celebrates 25 Years—Company Reflects on Silver Anniversary, Golden Future," July 2001; available at http://www.sas.com/news/preleases/071701/news1.html; retrieved December 5, 2001.

22. J. Schu, "Even in Hard Times, SAS Keeps Its Culture Intact," *Workforce* (October 2001): 21.

23. E. Chikofsky, "Would the People You Manage Hire You?" *IEEE Software* (March 1999): 98, 99.

24. K. Brooker, "Herb Kelleher: The Chairman of the Board Looks Back," *Fortune*, May 28, 2001, 62–76.

25. C. A. O'Reilly III and J. Pfeffer, "Southwest Airlines: If Success Is So Simple, Why Is It So Hard to Imitate?" in *Hidden Value: How Great Companies Achieve Extraordinary Results with Ordinary People*, ed. C. A. O'Reilly III and J. Pfeffer (Boston: Harvard Business School Press, 2000), 21–48.

26. E. Rasmusson, "Flying high: How Southwest Airlines Is Inspiring Loyalty in Trying Times," *Sales & Marketing Management* (December 2001): 55.

27. http://www.southwest.com; retrieved December 11, 2001.

28. Brooker, op. cit., 63, 64.

29. S. Carey and M. Trottman, "Three More Airlines Hit Stiff Head Wind," *Wall Street Journal*, April 19, 2002, A15.

30. http://www.southwest.com; retrieved on December 11, 2001.

31. O'Reilly and Pfeffer, "Southwest Airlines," op. cit.

32. H. Kelleher, quoted in Brooker, op. cit. 74.

33. Ibid.

34. Ibid., 33.

35. H. Kelleher, quoted in Brooker, op. cit. 72.

36. M. Ivins, "From Texas, with Love and Peanuts," *New York Times*, March 14, 1999, B11.

37. H. Kelleher, quoted in Brooker, op. cit., 72.

38. J. F. Parker, quoted in Conlin, op. cit.

39. "Best Employers in Asia 2001," *Hewitt Quarterly* 1, no. 3 (2001): 1–21.

40. Ibid., 14.

41. "The Costs of Downsizing versus the No-Layoff Payoff," *Business Week Online*, October 8, 2001; available at www.businessweek.com; retrieved October 13, 2001.

CHAPTER 7

1. *Merriam-Webster's New Collegiate Dictionary* (Springfield, MA: Merriam-Webster, 2001).

2. C. I. Barnard, *The Functions of the Executive* (Cambridge, MA: Harvard University Press, 1938).

3. J. Greenberg, "Reactions to Procedural Injustice in Payment Distributions: Do the Means Justify the Ends?" *Journal of Applied Psychology* 72 (1987): 55–61.

4. M. Kanovsky, "Understanding Procedural Justice and Its Impact on Business Organizations," *Journal of Management* 26 (2000): 489–511.

5. J. Greenberg, *The Quest for Justice on the Job* (Thousand Oaks, CA: Sage, 1997).

6. C. Maslach and M. Leiter, *The Truth about Burnout: How Organizations Cause Personal Stress and What to Do about It* (San Francisco: Jossey-Bass, 1997), 52.

7. M. Elovainio, M. Kivimaki, and K. Helkama, "Organizational Justice Evaluations, Job Control, and Occupational Strain," *Journal of Applied Psychology* 86 (2001): 418–424.

8. J. A. Colquitt, D. E. Conlon, M. J. Wesson, C. O. L. H. Porter, and K. Y. Ng, "Justice at the Millennium: A Meta-analytic Review of 25 Years of Organizational Justice Research," *Journal of Applied Psychology* 86 (2001): 425–445.

9. W. C. Borman and S. J. Motowidlo, "Expanding the Criterion Domain to Include Elements of Contextual Performance," in *Personnel Selection in Organizations,* ed. N. Schmitt and W. C. Borman (San Francisco: Jossey-Bass, 1993), 71–98.

10. R. H. Moorman, G. L. Blakely, and B. Niehoff, "Does Perceived Organizational Support Mediate the Relationship between Procedural Justice and Organizational Citizenship Behavior?" *Academy of Management Journal* 41 (1998): 351–357.

11. S. E. Naumann and N. Bennett, "A Case for Procedural Justice Climate: Development and Test of a Multilevel Model," *Academy of Management Journal* 43 (2000): 881–889.

12. Kanovsky, op. cit.

13. J. A. Colquitt, "On the Dimensionality of Organizational Justice: A Construct Validation of a Measure," *Journal of Applied Psychology* 86 (2001): 386–400.

14. R. J. Bies, "Interactional (In)justice: The Sacred and the Profane," in *Advances in Organizational Justice,* ed. J. Greenberg and R. Cropanzano (Lexington, MA: Lexington, 2001), 89–111.

15. S. S. Masterson, K. Lewis, B. M. Goldman, M. S. Taylor, "Integrating Justice and Social Exchange: The Differing Effects of Fair Procedures and Treatment on Work Relationships," *Academy of Management Journal* 43 (2000): 738–748.

16. C. Gopinath and T. E. Becker, "Communication, Procedural Justice, and Employee Attitudes: Relationships under Conditions of Divestiture," *Journal of Management* 26 (2000): 63–83.

17. A. K. Mishra and G. M. Spreitzer, "Explaining How Survivors Respond to Downsizing: The Roles of Trust, Empowerment, Justice, and Work Redesign," *Academy of Management Journal* 23 (1998): 567–588. See also J. Brockner and B. M. Wiesenfeld, "An Integrative

Framework for Explaining Reactions to Decisions: Interactive Effects of Outcomes and Procedures," *Psychological Bulletin* 120 (1996): 189–208.

18. D. M. Schweiger and A. S. DeNisi, "Communication with Employees Following a Merger: A Longitudinal Field Experiment," *Academy of Management Journal* 34 (1991): 110–135.

19. I computed the percentages in the table based on data from table 1 (time 3 and time 6) in ibid., 123.

20. J. Greenberg, "A Taxonomy of Organizational Justice Theories," *Academy of Management Review* 12 (1987): 9–22. See also J. Greenberg and R. Folger, "Procedural Justice, Participation, and the Fair Process Effect in Groups and Organizations," in *Basic Group Processes*, ed. B. Paulus (New York: Springer, 1983), 235–256.

21. M. Feldman and M. Spratt, *Five Frogs on a Log: A CEOs Field Guide to Accelerating the Transition in Mergers, Acquisitions, and Gut-Wrenching Change* (New York: Harper, 1999).

22. Ibid.

23. Ibid., 62, 67. See also R. Gray, "Internal Communication: Its Critical Role during Business Reorganizations," presentation to the Australian Human Resources Institute, Sydney, November 1, 2001.

24. Material in this section is based on G. Castles, as cited in Gray, ibid. See also R. D'Aprix, *Communicating for Change: Connecting the Workplace to the Marketplace* (San Francisco: Jossey-Bass, 1996); B. Quirke, *Communicating Corporate Change* (London: McGraw-Hill, 1996); J. D. Pincus and N. DeBonis, *Top Dog* (New York: McGraw-Hill, 1994); J. Shaffer, *The Leadership Solution* (New York: McGraw-Hill, 2000).

25. The broad framework for material in this section is based on the following sources: R. Cravotta and B. H. Kleiner, "New Developments Concerning Reductions in Force," *Management Research News* 24, nos. 3/4 (2001): 90–93; M. Moravec, "The Right Way to Rightsize," *Industry Week*, September 5, 1994, 46. See also W. F. Cascio, "Strategies for Responsible Restructuring," *Academy of Management Executive*, in press.

26. W. McKinley, J. Zhao, and K. G. Rust, "A Sociocognitive Interpretation of Organizational Downsizing," *Academy of Management Review* 25 (2000): 227–243.

27. "The Year Downsizing Grew Up," *The Economist*, December 21, 1996, 97–99.

28. M. Boyle, "How to Cut Perks without Killing Morale," *Fortune*, February 19, 2001, 241–244.

29. H. Mirvis, "Human Resource Management: Leaders, Laggards, and Followers," *Academy of Management Executive* 11, no. 2 (1997): 43–56.

30. K. E. Mishra, G. M. Spreitzer, and A. K. Mishra, "Preserving Employee Morale during Downsizing," *Sloan Management Review* 39, no. 2 (1998): 83–95.

31. J. Darling and R. Nurmi, "Downsizing the Multinational Firm: Key Variables for Excellence," *Leadership & Organization Development Journal* 16, no. 5 (1995): 22–28.

32. A. Barrionuevo, "Jobless in a Flash, Enron's Ex-employees Are Stunned, Bitter, Ashamed," *Wall Street Journal*, December 11, 2001, B1, B12.

33. W. F. Cascio, "Downsizing: What Do We Know? What Have We Learned?" *Academy of Management Executive* 7, no. 1 (1993): 95–104.

34. S. J. Appelbaum, A. Everard, and L. T. S. Hung, "Strategic Downsizing: Critical Success Factors," *Management Decision* 37, no. 7 (1999): 535–552.

35. T. H. Wagar, "Consequences of Work Force Reduction: Some Employer and Union Evidence," *Journal of Labor Research* 22, no. 4 (2001): 851–862.

36. Cascio, "Strategies for Responsible Restructuring."

37. M. F. R. Kets de Vries and K. Balazs, "The Downside of Downsizing," *Human Relations* 50, no. 1 (1997): 11–50.

38. Applebaum et al., op. cit.

39. Darling and Nurmi, op. cit.

Index

About the Author

 Wayne F. Cascio is a professor of management in the Graduate School of Business at the University of Colorado at Denver. He has been doing research and consulting on the topic of employment downsizing and restructuring for the past fifteen years. His article, "Downsizing: What Do We Know? What Have We Learned" won the Best Article award from the *Academy of Management Executive* in 1993, and it has been translated into many languages. In 1995 he wrote the U. S. Department of Labor's "Guide to Responsible Restructuring."

In collaboration with colleagues in finance and marketing, he published widely cited articles in 1997 and 1999 on the financial consequences of employment downsizing and restructuring in major U.S. corporations. Dr. Cascio has consulted with more than 150 organizations on six continents, His research on staffing, training, performance management, and the economic impact of human resource activities has appeared in a number of scholarly journals as well as those oriented toward practicing managers. Currently he serves on the Boards of Directors of CPP, Inc. and the Society for Human Resource Management Foundation

He is past president of the Society for Industrial and Organizational Psychology, and past Chair of the Human Resources Division of the Academy of Management. His previous books include *Man Human Resources: Productivity, Quality of Work Life, Profits* (6th ed., 2002), *Costing Human Resources: The Financial Impact of Behavior in Organizations* (4th ed., 2000); *Applied Psychology in Human Resource Management* (5th ed., 1998); *HR Planning, Employment, and Placement* (1989); and *Human Resource Management: An Information Systems Approach* (1981).

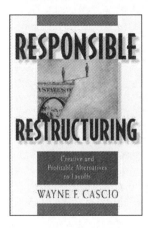

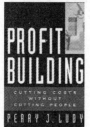

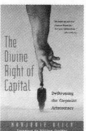